COLLECTIONS

Leveled Library

Teacher's Guide

Grade 2

Harcourt

Orlando Boston Dallas Chicago San Diego

Visit *The Learning Site!*
www.harcourtschool.com

The Leveled Libraries Chart is intended to help Reading Recovery® teachers in purchasing leveled books from Harcourt. Please note the following:

(1) Reading Recovery® is a registered service mark of The Ohio State University.

(2) The complete Reading Recovery® book list, created by the Reading Recovery® Council of North America, includes books from numerous publishers since a premise of the program is that children be provided with a wide range of texts. One publisher's book list alone is not sufficient to implement a Reading Recovery® program.

(3) Levels are subject to change as they are periodically tested and reevaluated.

Printed in the United States of America

ISBN 0-15-313632-4

1 2 3 4 5 6 7 8 9 10 073 2003 2002 2001 2000

Contents

Leveled Library Books

Leveled Library books are trade books that have been leveled using a consistent formula across all grades. The libraries at each grade offer a range of reading levels, starting with books written at approximately one grade level below a particular grade level and increasing in difficulty to include books written two grade levels above. Leveled Library books make it possible to match students to texts with which they will be successful. Benchmark Books are also provided to periodically assess students' progress.

How the Books Were Leveled

Certain characteristics of a book can be strong indicators of its ease or difficulty. At the primary grades, these characteristics were included in the leveling process:

- content
- illustrations
- vocabulary
- repetition of language patterns
- language structures
- narrative structure
- text position

At the intermediate grades, the criteria were expanded to include:

- prior knowledge
- vocabulary and vocabulary concepts
- amount of text
- length of book
- text structure
- genre
- illustration support

Benchmark Books

Benchmark Books are Leveled Library books specially selected to represent levels of reading difficulty within a grade. Six Benchmark Books are provided to mark your students' reading progress at various times during the school year.

Using the Benchmark Books for Evaluation

Two forms accompany each Benchmark Book—the Benchmark Book Individual Reading Inventory Form and the Individual Reading Inventory Summary Form.

- The Benchmark Book Individual Reading Inventory Form contains text from the book and a set of comprehension questions.
- The Individual Reading Inventory Summary Form provides a framework for recording and analyzing a student's performance.

A teacher has three options based upon the Benchmark Book evaluation.

- If the student reads the book with almost perfect accuracy, reassess him or her at a higher level.
- If the student meets the benchmark, he or she is ready to begin reading instruction at that level.
- If the student makes too many errors, reassess him or her at a lower level.

Guided Reading Groups

Students reading at the same level can be assigned to guided reading groups. Within these groups, the teacher can support the students' use of strategies by modeling and encouraging the things that good readers do, such as

- thinking about whether a word makes sense
- self-correcting
- using word parts or known words to decode unfamiliar words

Working within the range of the Leveled Library books, all students can progress, level by level, toward becoming fluent, lifelong readers.

Individual Reading Inventory

The six Benchmark Books in the Leveled Library, in addition to their regular four-page lessons, are accompanied by a two-page Individual Reading Inventory (IRI) feature. These features occur in the back of this book on pages 104–109.

What Is an IRI?

An Individual Reading Inventory is an assessment tool to help a teacher learn about a child's reading strategies and to help plan instruction. While a student is reading aloud, the teacher records everything he or she says or does. An IRI has two primary parts: a reading passage and comprehension questions.

Administering the IRI

1. Before reading, explain the task. Tell the student that he or she will read a passage aloud and then answer four questions.
2. During reading, unobtrusively record oral miscues on the Individual Reading Inventory Form. Use the Marking Oral Miscues chart to record oral errors and self-corrections.
3. After reading, ask the student the questions at the bottom of the Individual Reading Inventory Form. Mark correct (+) and incorrect (-) responses.

Miscues

Total the number of miscues and self-corrections. Then follow the steps on the Individual Reading Inventory Summary Form to compute the Error Rate. Look for an Error Rate of 10% or less to confirm instructional reading level, and 5% or less to confirm independent reading level.

Error Rate

1. Total the number of miscues.
2. Subtract the total number of self-corrections from the total number of miscues for a subtotal.
3. Divide this subtotal by the word count of the passage.

Fluency

Count the number of words read correctly in one minute. Count repetitions and self-corrections as correctly read words. Look for the following ranges of correctly read words per minute:

- 40–60 by the end of grade one
- 60–90 by the end of grade two
- 80–100 by the end of grade three
- 100–120 by the end of grade four
- 100–130 by the end of grade five
- 120–140 by the end of grade six

Comprehension

Total the number of correct responses to the questions. Look for a score of 75% or higher to confirm instructional reading level. To help evaluate comprehension errors, questions 1 and 2 require literal thinking, and questions 3 and 4 require inferential thinking.

Marking Oral Reading Miscues

READING MISCUE	MARKING	SAMPLE
1. Omissions	Circle the word, word part, or phrase omitted.	I will let you go in.
2. Insertions	Insert a caret (^) and write in the inserted word or phrase.	big We bought a ^ parrot.
3. Substitutions	Write the word or phrase the student substitutes above the word or phrase in the text.	the Dad fixed ~~my~~ bike.
4. Mispronunciations	Write the phonetic mispronunciation above the word.	feed Have you ~~fed~~ the dog?
5. Self-corrections	Write the letters SC next to the miscue that is self-corrected.	We took our space. SC
6. Repetitions	Draw a line under any part of the text that is repeated.	It is your garden garden now.
7. Punctuation	Circle punctuation missed. Write in any punctuation inserted.	Take them home. Then come back, and you and I will go to town.
8. Hesitations	Place vertical lines at places where the student hesitates excessively.	Pretend / this is mine.

Leveled Libraries Chart

Books in the *Leveled Libraries* overlap across the grade levels. The following chart shows the placement of the *Leveled Library* books for Grade 2.

Book Title	Leveled Library Level	Reading Recovery® Level	Guided Reading Level	Strategies Good Readers Use
What Do You Like?	1.0–1.5	3–4	B	Self-Correct; Use Prior Knowledge; Make and Confirm Predictions
Flying	1.0–1.5	7–8	D–E	Use Picture Clues to Confirm Meaning; Create Mental Images; Make and Confirm Predictions
Good Night, Sigmund	1.5–2.0	3–4	F–I	Reread Aloud; Use Picture Clues to Confirm Meaning; Make and Confirm Predictions
The Happy Day	1.5–2.0	13–14	F–I	Use Picture Clues to Confirm Meaning; Create Mental Images; Self-Correct
The Best Friends Club	2.0	29–30	J	Look at Word Bits and Parts; Reread; Make and Confirm Predictions
Amelia Bedelia Helps Out	2.0–2.5		J–L	Reread; Sequence Events/Summmarize; Use Picture Clues to Confirm Meaning
For Pete's Sake	2.0–2.5		J–L	Create Mental Images; Use Picture Clues to Confirm Meaning; Self-Correct
There's a Dragon In My Sleeping Bag	2.0–2.5		J–L	Look at Word Bits and Parts; Sequence Events/ Summarize; Reread
The Rooster Who Went To His Uncle's Wedding	2.0–2.5		J–L	Self-Correct; Sequence Events/Summarize; Make and Confirm Predictions
Little Polar Bear and the Brave Little Hare	2.0–2.5		J–L	Create Mental Images; Sequence Events/ Summarize; Make and Confirm Predictions
Alistair In Outer Space	2.5		L	Look at Word Bits and Parts; Self-Correct; Create Mental Images
Who's Who in My Family?	2.5–3.0		L–M	Use Prior Knowledge; Self-Correct; Look at Word Bits and Parts
Flowers, Fruits, Seeds	2.5–3.0		L–M	Reread; Use Picture Clues to Confirm Meaning; Sequence Events/Summarize
The Leaving Morning	2.5–3.0		L–M	Use Prior Knowledge; Use Picture Clues to Confirm Meaning; Make and Confirm Predictions
Grandpa Takes Me to the Moon	2.5–3.0		L–M	Use Context to Confirm Meaning; Self-Correct; Create Mental Images
Emergency!	3.0		M–N	Reread; Use Picture Clues to Confirm Meaning; Self-Correct
Stellaluna	3.0–3.5		N–O	Look at Word Bits and Parts; Look for Words You Know; Make and Confirm Predictions
The Puddle Pail	3.0–3.5		N–O	Reread; Use Picture Clues to Confirm Meaning; Make and Confirm Predictions
The Little Painter of Sabana Grande	3.0–3.5		N–O	Reread; Make Inferences; Self-Correct
Julian, Dream Doctor	3.0–3.5		N–O	Read ahead; Use Prior Knowledge; Make and Confirm Predictions
Pablo's Tree	3.0–3.5		N–O	Read ahead; Sequence Events/ Summarize; Look for Words You Know
Out of the Ocean	3.5+		O–P	Create Mental Images; Use Picture Clues to Confirm Meaning; Make and Confirm Predictions
Cam Jansen and the Mystery of Flight 54	3.5+		O–P	Reread; Create Mental Images; Make and Confirm Predictions
Happy Birthday, Martin Luther King	3.5+		O–P	Reread; Self-Correct; Sequence Events/ Summarize

Reading Level

Summary

In this overview of airplane flight, people board the plane. Then it taxis to the runway, gets ready, and takes off into the sky. It flies over the airport and then over highways, rivers, and cities. It flies across the country, over mountains, and into and over the clouds. Then it flies down and lands at another airport.

Author/Illustrator Information

Donald Crews welcomes opportunities to visit and talk with people who enjoy his work—children, parents, teachers, and librarians. He says, "I don't begin any new project without thinking about this audience; . . . they inspire me." Crews writes and illustrates his own books, and he illustrates books by other authors. His work has won many awards.

More Books by Donald Crews

Truck

Sail Away

Night at the Fair

School Bus

Harbor

Parade

Flying

by Donald Crews

Introducing the Book

You may wish to ask children the following questions to **build background** and to **introduce story vocabulary.**

- What could you see if you looked down from a flying plane?
- What is an airport?
- What does boarding a plane mean? If you have done it, what do you remember about it?
- What is a runway? What does it look like?
- What is a plane doing when it's taxiing onto a runway?

SETTING A PURPOSE Display the book cover and show children the first few pictures. Tell children that one purpose for reading is to learn about something. Have them set a purpose for reading *Flying*. If children have difficulty setting a purpose, offer this suggestion:

> MODEL **The title and pictures tell me this book is about flying in an airplane. I'll read to learn more about what it is like to fly in an airplane.**

Reading Options

DIRECTED READING Use the Monitor Comprehension questions and Guided Reading strategies on pages 9–10 to check children's comprehension. WHOLE CLASS/SMALL GROUP

INDEPENDENT READING Have children read *Flying* and complete the comprehension questions on page 11 independently. Encourage children to write their reactions to the story in their Reading Logs. INDIVIDUAL/WHOLE CLASS

Monitor Comprehension

Use these questions to monitor children's comprehension and to evaluate their use of reading strategies.

Pages 2–9

1. **What happens before the plane taxis to the runway?** (People board the plane.) LITERAL: SEQUENCE
2. **What do the pictures on pages 4–5 and 6–7 tell you about why the plane has to wait on the runway?** (Possible response: Each plane has to wait for its turn to take off.) INFERENTIAL: USE PICTURE CLUES
3. **What do you think the people on the plane are doing while they wait for takeoff?** (Possible response: sitting in their seats; thinking about where they are going; feeling nervous, excited, or bored) INFERENTIAL: SPECULATE

Guided Reading

FOCUS STRATEGY **USE PICTURE CLUES TO CONFIRM MEANING** Point out to children that the pictures in a story can help them make sure they read the words correctly. Suggest that they look at the pictures in this story to help them make sure they correctly read the words about flying.

Monitor Comprehension

Pages 10–17

4. **What can people on the plane see on the ground as the plane is flying?** (Possible response: buildings, cars, trucks, boats, roads, and rivers) LITERAL: NOTE DETAILS
5. **Why are the buildings and bridges in the pictures smaller than the plane?** (Possible response: The picture shows what it might look like from high up in a plane; from the sky, everything on the ground looks small.) INFERENTIAL: DETERMINE ILLUSTRATOR'S PURPOSE
6. **How can you make sure you have read the words on page 17 correctly?** (Possible response: look at the picture to make sure) INFERENTIAL: USE PICTURE CLUES

Guided Reading

FOCUS STRATEGY **CREATE MENTAL IMAGES** If children have difficulty understanding why things on the ground look so much smaller than the airplane, tell them that they can create a picture in their minds to help them. Ask: **Have you ever looked down from a high place? What did things on the ground look like?**

Monitor Comprehension

Pages 18–25

7. **Where is the plane going on its trip?** (across the country) LITERAL: NOTE DETAILS
8. **What large things does the plane fly over?** (mountains) LITERAL: NOTE DETAILS
9. **What do you think clouds look like from an airplane?** (Possible responses: white or dark; like cotton balls; like wool) INFERENTIAL: USE PICTURE CLUES

Guided Reading

FOCUS STRATEGY **MAKE AND CONFIRM PREDICTIONS** Give children an opportunity to predict what will happen in the next part of the story.

Monitor Comprehension

Pages 26–33

10. **Where does the plane land?** (at another airport) LITERAL: NOTE DETAILS
11. **How long does the trip take? Look back at the pictures to help you decide.** (Possible responses: one day; the story starts in daylight and the last pictures show night time) INFERENTIAL: USE PICTURE CLUES
12. **What helps the plane land safely at night?** (Possible response: lights on the plane, at the airport, and on the runway) INFERENTIAL: DRAW CONCLUSIONS

RETELLING Guidelines for performing a retelling of the story, as well as a rubric for evaluating the retelling, are provided on pages 110–111 of this teacher's guide.

ANSWERS TO COMPREHENSION QUESTIONS ON PAGE 11:

1. (Possible responses: boarding, taxiing, takeoff, flying, landing) INFERENTIAL: SUMMARIZE
2. (Responses will vary.) CRITICAL: EXPRESS PERSONAL OPINIONS
3. (Possible response: Flying is faster than driving by car or sailing by ship.) CRITICAL: LITERARY ANALYSIS

Response to the Literature

WRITING Children should use vocabulary and concepts from *Flying* as they write their own story about taking a trip on an airplane. They should use complete sentences.

Name ______________________________

Flying

Write answers to these questions.

1. Name, in order, five things that happen on a plane trip.

____

____

____

2. Would you like to fly on an airplane? Why or why not?

____

____

____

3. When people have to travel far, why is it good to fly?

____

____

____

RESPONSE TO THE LITERATURE

WRITING Imagine that you are going to fly on an airplane. On another sheet of paper, write a story about what happens on your trip. Write about boarding the plane, taking off, flying, and landing. Use complete sentences.

Reading Level

Summary

What do you like? This question is answered by two children. Though they both like the same things, the illustrations show each child's specific preference in each category. For example, though both children like fruit, one prefers apples, while the other prefers watermelons. When it comes to music, one thinks of a piano and of birds singing, while the other thinks of the sound of a flute. When both say they love their mother, the illustrations reveal that they have the same mother. Finally, the reader is asked what he or she likes and loves.

Author/Illustrator Information

Michael Grejniec was born in Poland. He has written and illustrated several books. Some of his books have been published in Spanish.

More Books by Michael Grejniec

¿Que te gusta? (translation of *What Do You Like?*)

Good Morning, Good Night/ Buenos días, buenas noches

When I Open My Eyes

Albert's Nap

Look

What Do You Like?

by Michael Grejniec

Introducing the Book

You may wish to ask children the following questions to **build background** and **introduce story vocabulary.**

- Have you ever seen a rainbow? What did it look like?
- What games do you like to play?
- What fruit do you most like to eat?
- What kind of music do you like to listen to?

SETTING A PURPOSE Display the book cover, read aloud the title, and show children the first two pictures. Read the text on these pages, and point out that two children are taking turns saying what they like. Tell children that one reason for reading is to learn about others. Have children set a purpose for reading *What Do You Like?* If they have difficulty setting a purpose, offer this suggestion:

> MODEL **These pictures show different ways people think about the same thing. I'll read to find out what the children in the story think of when they say they like something.**

Reading Options

DIRECTED READING Use the Monitor Comprehension questions and Guided Reading strategies on pages 13–14 to check children's comprehension. WHOLE CLASS/SMALL GROUP

INDEPENDENT READING Have children read *What Do You Like?* and complete the comprehension questions on page 15 independently. Encourage children to write their reactions to the story in their Reading Logs. INDIVIDUAL/WHOLE CLASS

Monitor Comprehension

Use these questions to monitor children's comprehension and to evaluate their use of reading strategies.

Pages 2–9

1. **How are the rainbows that the children in the story think of the same? How are they different?** (Possible response: Both rainbows are colorful. One rainbow looks like a real rainbow; the other rainbow looks like a drawing of a rainbow.) INFERENTIAL: COMPARE AND CONTRAST
2. **What does each child like to play with?** (a ball; boomerangs) LITERAL: NOTE DETAILS
3. **How is playing ball different from playing with a boomerang? How are they alike?** (Possible response: People can play ball alone or with others; boomerangs are played with alone. Both are fun to play with.) INFERENTIAL: COMPARE AND CONTRAST

Guided Reading

FOCUS STRATEGY **SELF-CORRECT** Tell children that sometimes when they don't read a word correctly, they might notice that the letters in the word do not match the way they have read it. Have children correct themselves when this happens by looking carefully at the word and rereading it.

Monitor Comprehension

Pages 10–17

4. **What kind of cat does each child like?** (One likes a pet cat; the other likes a tiger.) LITERAL: NOTE DETAILS
5. **Why do you think the children's ideas about cats are different?** (Possible response: One may have a pet cat; the other may think tigers are more interesting.) INFERENTIAL: SPECULATE
6. **What kind of fruit does each child like?** (One likes apples; the other likes watermelon.) LITERAL: NOTE DETAILS

Guided Reading

FOCUS STRATEGY **USE PRIOR KNOWLEDGE** If children have difficulty understanding the connection between the text about music and flying and the illustrations depicting aspects of those concepts, point out that they can use what they already know about music and flying to help them.

Monitor Comprehension

Pages 18–25

7. **What sounds of music does each child like?** (Possible response: One likes playing a piano and hearing birds singing; the other likes the sound of a flute.) INFERENTIAL: USE PICTURE CLUES
8. **What sounds of music do you like?** (Responses will vary.) CRITICAL: EXPRESS PERSONAL OPINIONS
9. **Which way would you like to fly?** (Responses will vary.) CRITICAL: EXPRESS PERSONAL OPINIONS

Guided Reading

FOCUS STRATEGY **MAKE AND CONFIRM PREDICTIONS** Tell children that they can make and confirm predictions to help them understand a story better. Have them use story clues in pictures and text and what they know from real life to think about what might happen next. After reading, they can compare their predictions to what really happened.

Monitor Comprehension

Pages 26–29

10. **Who do both children love?** (their mother) LITERAL: NOTE DETAILS
11. **Whose mother do you think is in the picture on page 27?** (Responses will vary.) INFERENTIAL: MAKE PREDICTIONS
12. **Whose mother is she? How do you know?** (Possible response: She is the mother of both children. She is hugging both of them.) METACOGNITIVE: CONFIRM PREDICTIONS

RETELLING Guidelines for performing a retelling of the story, as well as a rubric for evaluating the retelling, are provided on pages 110–111 of this teacher's guide.

ANSWERS TO COMPREHENSION QUESTIONS ON PAGE 15:

1. (Possible responses: They both like the rainbow, to play, their cats, fruit, music, to fly; they both love their mother.) INFERENTIAL: SUMMARIZE
2. (Responses will vary.) CRITICAL: EXPRESS PERSONAL OPINIONS
3. (Possible response: They have the same mother; they must be brother and sister.) CRITICAL: LITERARY ANALYSIS

Response to the Literature

WRITING Children should write complete sentences. They may want to assemble their pages to create a picture book titled "What I Like."

Name ______________________________

What Do You Like?

Answer with complete sentences.

1. What do the children in this book both like and both love?

____

____

____

2. What do you like?

____

____

____

3. What do you find out about the two children at the end of the story?

____

____

____

RESPONSE TO THE LITERATURE

WRITING Think about things you like and people you love. Use a separate page for each idea. Draw pictures of what you like and people you love. On each page, write a complete sentence about the picture.

Reading Level

Summary

Hello, Sigmund. No matter what Sigmund's owner does, or where he goes, Sigmund the cat is there. That is, until bedtime, when Sigmund can't be found. Suddenly, he reappears, just in time to say good night. Good night, Sigmund.

Author/Illustrator Information

Nancy Coffelt got the inspiration for *Good Night, Sigmund* from the real Sigmund, a big, gray, lovable cat. The house Ms. Coffelt shares with her family in Portland, Oregon, has always been filled with animals. *Good Night, Sigmund* is Nancy Coffelt's first book for children. She has also illustrated a book for adults who are nervous about traveling by plane.

More Books by Nancy Coffelt

Dogs in Space

Tom's Fish

The Dog Who Cried Woof

Good Night, Sigmund

by Nancy Coffelt

Introducing the Book

You may wish to ask children the following questions to **build background** and **introduce story vocabulary.**

- When do you wear slippers?
- What do you like to eat for breakfast?
- What is the weather like outside today?
- When would you wear a raincoat?
- What do you like to eat for dinner?
- When is your bedtime?

SETTING A PURPOSE Display the book cover, read aloud the title, and show children the first few pictures. Tell children that one reason for reading is to be entertained. Have children set a purpose for reading *Good Night, Sigmund.* If they have difficulty setting a purpose, offer this suggestion:

> **MODEL** **These pictures show that there is a cat in this story. I'll read to find out what the cat does.**

Reading Options

DIRECTED READING Use the Monitor Comprehension questions and Guided Reading strategies on pages 17–18 to check children's comprehension. WHOLE CLASS/SMALL GROUP

INDEPENDENT READING Have children read *Good Night, Sigmund* and complete the comprehension questions on page 19 independently. Encourage children to write their reactions to the story in their Reading Logs. INDIVIDUAL/WHOLE CLASS

Monitor Comprehension

Use these questions to monitor children's comprehension and to evaluate their use of reading strategies.

Pages 2–5

1. **What are the first two things the boy does after he gets up in the morning?** (He puts on his slippers and eats breakfast.) LITERAL: SEQUENCE
2. **What does Sigmund do with the boy's slippers?** (Possible response: He plays with them.) INFERENTIAL: USE PICTURE CLUES
3. **Does Sigmund act like a real cat? How do you know?** (Possible response: No. He can hold bananas and a glass; real cats cannot do this.) METACOGNITIVE: USE PRIOR KNOWLEDGE

Guided Reading

FOCUS STRATEGY **REREAD ALOUD** Tell children that when they stop at a new word while reading, they can reread the sentence aloud. Encourage children to reread aloud when they come to words they do not know.

Monitor Comprehension

Pages 6–15

4. **What does the boy do on a sunny day?** (He goes outside and plays on the swings.) LITERAL: NOTE DETAILS
5. **What five things can the boy do on a rainy day?** (He can put on a raincoat and go outside, build a tower, drive a dump truck, talk to his bears, or just sit.) LITERAL: NOTE DETAILS
6. **Does Sigmund like the boy? How do you know?** (Possible response: Yes, Sigmund is always with the boy.) METACOGNITIVE: DETERMINE CHARACTERS' EMOTIONS

Guided Reading

FOCUS STRATEGY **USE PICTURE CLUES TO CONFIRM MEANING** Point out to children that the pictures in a story can help them make sure they read the words correctly. Suggest to children that they look at the pictures in this story to help them make sure they did.

Monitor Comprehension

Pages 16–21

7. **What is the first thing the boy does after dinner?** (He takes a bath.) LITERAL: SEQUENCE
8. **Do you think a real cat would sit in the bathtub? Why or why not?** (Possible response: probably not; because most cats do not like water) INFERENTIAL: CAUSE-EFFECT
9. **Where do you think Sigmund is when it is time for bed?** (Responses will vary.) INFERENTIAL: SPECULATE

Guided Reading

FOCUS STRATEGY **MAKE AND CONFIRM PREDICTIONS** Remind children that they can use story clues and what they know from real life to think about what might happen next. After reading, they can compare their predictions to what really happened.

Monitor Comprehension

Pages 22–25

10. **Where does Sigmund turn up? Where was he hiding?** (Possible response: Sigmund turns up on the boy's bed. He was hiding under the covers.) INFERENTIAL: CONFIRM PREDICTIONS

11. **How do you think Nancy Coffelt, the author and illustrator of this story, feels about cats?** (Possible response: I think she likes cats. Sigmund and the boy really seem to like each other.) METACOGNITIVE: INTERPRET AUTHOR'S VIEWPOINT

RETELLING Guidelines for performing a retelling of the story, as well as a rubric for evaluating the retelling, are provided on pages 110–111 of this teacher's guide.

ANSWERS TO COMPREHENSION QUESTIONS ON PAGE 19:

1. (Possible response: Sigmund and the boy spend the day together. They play on the swings, walk in the rain, play inside with toys, sit, take a bath, and go to sleep.) INFERENTIAL: SUMMARIZE
2. (Responses will vary.) CRITICAL: PERSONAL RESPONSE
3. (Possible response: Sigmund is like a real cat because he looks like a cat, he plays with slippers, he follows the boy around, he jumps, and he hides. Sigmund is different from a real cat when he holds bananas, a glass of juice, and an umbrella; when he likes rain and taking a bath; and when he winks.) CRITICAL: LITERARY ANALYSIS

Response to the Literature

WRITING Children should use a morning-to-night sequence similar to that in *Good Night, Sigmund*. They should write in complete sentences and a paragraph format.

Name ______________________________

Good Night, Sigmund

Write complete sentences to answer each question.

1. What do the boy and Sigmund do together?

____

____

____

2. Would you like to have a cat like Sigmund? Why or why not?

____

____

____

3. How is Sigmund like a real cat? How is he different from a real cat?

____

____

____

RESPONSE TO THE LITERATURE

WRITING Imagine spending a whole day with a pet. On another sheet of paper, write a story about what the two of you could do together. Use complete sentences and a paragraph format.

Reading Level

Summary

As snow falls, the forest animals sleep: field mice, bears, snails, squirrels, and groundhogs. One by one, they awake, sniff the air, leave their cozy beds, and run. Suddenly, they stop to admire a flower growing in the snow.

Author and Illustrator Information

Ruth Krauss has said, "I have had no special training in writing . . ." and feels that her writing is closely tied to her training in art and music. Her books, however, are illustrated by other people, including her husband, Crockett Johnson, creator of *Harold and the Purple Crayon.*

Marc Simont has illustrated more than 50 books by other authors, including the *Nate the Great* series by Marjorie Weinman Sharmat. *The Happy Day* was named a Caldecott Honor book.

More Books by Ruth Krauss

The Carrot Seed
I'll Be You and You Be Me

The Happy Day

by Ruth Krauss

illustrated by Marc Simont

Introducing the Book

You may wish to ask children the following questions to **build background** and **introduce story vocabulary.**

- What is snow? What is it like?
- What do animals look like when they are sleeping?
- What do you think field mice are?
- Where do bears live?
- What do snails look like?
- What do squirrels eat?
- What are groundhogs? Where do they live?
- What does sniff mean?

SETTING A PURPOSE Display the book cover and ask children to read the title aloud. Then show children the first few pictures. Tell children that one reason for reading is to learn new things. Have children set a purpose for reading *The Happy Day*. If they have difficulty setting a purpose, offer this suggestion:

> MODEL **I can see a lot of animals in the story. I'll read to find out what they are, where they live, and what they do.**

Reading Options

DIRECTED READING Use the Monitor Comprehension questions and Guided Reading strategies on pages 21–22 to check children's comprehension. WHOLE CLASS/SMALL GROUP

INDEPENDENT READING Have children read *The Happy Day* and complete the comprehension questions on page 23 independently. Encourage children to write their reactions to the story in their Reading Logs. INDIVIDUAL/WHOLE CLASS

Monitor Comprehension

Use these questions to monitor children's comprehension and to evaluate their use of reading strategies.

Pages 2–9

1. **What animals are in this story?** (field mice, bears, snails, squirrels, and groundhogs) LITERAL: NOTE DETAILS
2. **Where do the animals sleep?** (Possible response: The mice sleep under the snow; the bears sleep in caves.) INFERENTIAL: DRAW CONCLUSIONS
3. **Why do you think these animals sleep through the winter?** (Possible responses: There's not much food; it's cold and snowy outside.) INFERENTIAL: CAUSE-EFFECT

Guided Reading

FOCUS STRATEGY **USE PICTURE CLUES TO CONFIRM MEANING** Ask children how they can make sure they have read unfamiliar words in this story correctly. (They can look for picture clues.) For example, on page 8 they can make sure they read the word *squirrels* correctly by looking at the picture to find out what is sleeping in the trees.

Monitor Comprehension

Pages 10–17

4. **What do all the animals do after they open their eyes?** (They sniff.) LITERAL: NOTE DETAILS
5. **Why do you think all the animals sniff?** (Possible responses: They smell something interesting; animals sniff for food or danger.) INFERENTIAL: SPECULATE
6. **What do you think will happen next?** (Responses will vary.) INFERENTIAL: MAKE PREDICTIONS

Guided Reading

FOCUS STRATEGY **CREATE MENTAL IMAGES** Point out to children that sometimes they can understand a story better when they picture in their minds what is happening. Suggest that they imagine each of the animals in the story sniffing and think about why they might be doing this.

Monitor Comprehension

Pages 18–25

7. **What do all the animals do next?** (They run.) LITERAL: SEQUENCE

8. **What have you learned about the animals by reading this story?** (Responses will vary.) INFERENTIAL: IMPORTANT DETAILS

9. **What do you think the animals are running toward?** (Responses will vary.) INFERENTIAL: MAKE PREDICTIONS

Guided Reading

FOCUS STRATEGY **MAKE AND CONFIRM PREDICTIONS** Give children the opportunity to predict what will happen at the end of the story.

Monitor Comprehension

Pages 26–29

10. **How close did your prediction come to what happened?** (Responses will vary.) INFERENTIAL: CONFIRM PREDICTIONS

11. **Why are the animals so happy to see the flower?** (Possible response: The flower means spring is coming, bringing warmer weather and more food.) INFERENTIAL: DRAW CONCLUSIONS

12. **How is the illustration on the last page of the book different from all the other illustrations? Why do you think the illustrator made it different?** (Possible response: The last illustration is the only one that has color. The illustrator wanted to show that a colorful spring comes after a dull winter.) INFERENTIAL: DETERMINE ILLUSTRATOR'S PURPOSE

RETELLING Guidelines for performing a retelling of the story, as well as a rubric for evaluating the retelling, are provided on pages 110–111 of this teacher's guide.

ANSWERS TO COMPREHENSION QUESTIONS ON PAGE 23:

1. (Possible response: They wake up, sniff, run, and find a yellow flower in the snow. They are happy spring is here.) INFERENTIAL: SUMMARIZE

2. (Responses will vary.) CRITICAL: EXPRESS PERSONAL OPINIONS

3. (Possible response: The story is about a happy day for the animals, the day they wake up and discover it is spring.) INFERENTIAL: DETERMINE AUTHOR'S PURPOSE

Response to the Literature

WRITING Each story should tell about the child's own happy day. Ideally, the story should have a surprise at the end. Children should use complete sentences.

Name ______________________

The Happy Day

Answer with complete sentences.

1. What do the animals in this story do?

____

____

____

2. How do you feel at the end of winter and the beginning of spring?

____

____

____

3. Why is *The Happy Day* a good title for this story?

____

____

____

Harcourt

RESPONSE TO THE LITERATURE

WRITING On another sheet of paper, write a story about a day that was happy for you. You might call your story "My Happy Day." Try to have a surprise at the end, like the flower in *The Happy Day*. Write in complete sentences.

Reading Level

Summary

Lizzie and Harold are best friends who form a two-person club that meets under Lizzie's porch. When Harold becomes friends with Douglas, Lizzie feels left out. She writes new club rules that force Harold to choose between Douglas and the club. Harold quits the club—but then he and Douglas convince Lizzie to be friends with them both. Together they form a new club, "The No Rules Club."

Author and Illustrator Information

Elizabeth Winthrop began writing when she was 12. Believing that "writing is ten percent talent and ninety percent practice and perseverance," she tries to write something every day, whether a letter, a journal entry, or part of a story. She has written many books, most for children; her best-known title is probably *The Castle in the Attic.*

Martha Weston has illustrated dozens of books for children and teachers. She and her family live in northern California.

More Books by Elizabeth Winthrop

As the Crow Flies

Maggie and the Monster

Shoes

A Very Noisy Girl

The Best Friends Club

by Elizabeth Winthrop
illustrated by Martha Weston

Introducing the Book

You may wish to ask children the following questions to **build background** and **introduce story vocabulary.**

- What is a clubhouse?
- What does it mean to be members of a group?
- When someone is president of something, what does that mean?
- What does a vice president do?
- Why are rules important when you are playing a game?
- What does it mean to quit something?
- How can a sign help you?

SETTING A PURPOSE Display the book cover and ask children to read aloud the title. Tell children that one reason for reading is for enjoyment. Have children set a purpose for reading *The Best Friends Club.* If they have difficulty setting a purpose, offer this suggestion:

> MODEL **The title tells me this book is about a club for best friends. I'll read to find out who the best friends are and what their club is like.**

Reading Options

DIRECTED READING Use the Monitor Comprehension questions and Guided Reading strategies on pages 25–26 to check children's comprehension. WHOLE CLASS/SMALL GROUP

INDEPENDENT READING Have children read *The Best Friends Club* and complete the comprehension questions on page 27 independently. Encourage children to write their reactions to the story in their Reading Logs. INDIVIDUAL/WHOLE CLASS

Monitor Comprehension

Use these questions to monitor children's comprehension and to evaluate their use of reading strategies.

Pages 1–7

1. **Why do you think Harold and Lizzie are best friends?** (Possible response: They play together, teach each other things, share, and like the same things.) INFERENTIAL: DRAW CONCLUSIONS
2. **Whose idea is it to start a best friends club?** (Lizzie's) LITERAL: NOTE DETAILS
3. **What are the rules of the club?** (The club meets under Lizzie's porch, no one else can be in the club, Lizzie and Harold walk home from school together every day, and everyone in the club knows cat's cradle.) INFERENTIAL: SUMMARIZE

Guided Reading

FOCUS STRATEGY **LOOK AT WORD BITS AND PARTS** Tell children that one way to figure out an unfamiliar word is to look for smaller words they know inside the longer word. Children may apply this strategy to reading words such as *clubhouse*, *painted*, and *everybody*.

Monitor Comprehension

Pages 8–15

4. **Why won't Lizzie let Douglas walk home with her and Harold?** (One of the club rules is that just Harold and Lizzie walk home together.) LITERAL: NOTE DETAILS
5. **How does Lizzie feel about Douglas? How do you know?** (Possible response: She doesn't seem to like him. She says unkind things about him, writes new club rules, sticks out her tongue at Harold and Douglas, and throws a ball at the garage.) METACOGNITIVE: DETERMINE CHARACTERS' EMOTIONS
6. **What does Lizzie mean when she says Douglas's shoelaces are "dripping"?** (Possible response: His shoelaces are untied.) INFERENTIAL: UNDERSTAND FIGURATIVE LANGUAGE

Guided Reading

FOCUS STRATEGY **REREAD** Ask children what they should do if they aren't sure what has happened in a story. (Go back and read it again, slowly and carefully.) Point out that rereading portions of a selection may help them understand it better.

Monitor Comprehension

Pages 16–23

7. **Why does Harold quit the club?** (Harold says the club is no fun because it has too many rules.) LITERAL: NOTE DETAILS
8. **How do you know that Harold still likes Lizzie?** (Possible response: He comes back with Douglas to talk to Lizzie about a three-person club.) METACOGNITIVE: DETERMINE CHARACTERS' EMOTIONS
9. **Why do you think Lizzie comes out from under the porch?** (Possible response: She is lonely and decides it would be more fun to play.) INFERENTIAL: DETERMINE CHARACTERS' EMOTIONS
10. **What do you think will happen next?** (Responses will vary.) INFERENTIAL: MAKE PREDICTIONS

Guided Reading

FOCUS STRATEGY **MAKE AND CONFIRM PREDICTIONS** Give children the opportunity to predict what will happen next in the story.

Monitor Comprehension

Pages 24–30

11. **Why does Lizzie change her mind about the club?** (Possible responses: She sees that Douglas is nice; she doesn't want to lose Harold's friendship.) INFERENTIAL: DRAW CONCLUSIONS
12. **Do you think "The No Rules Club" is a good name for the new club? Explain your answer.** (Responses will vary.) CRITICAL: EXPRESS PERSONAL OPINIONS
13. **How do you know that Lizzie and Harold are still best friends?** (They both go to Lizzie's house for supper; they are holding hands in the illustration.) METACOGNITIVE: DRAW CONCLUSIONS

RETELLING Guidelines for performing a retelling of the story, as well as a rubric for evaluating the retelling, are provided on pages 110–111 of this teacher's guide.

ANSWERS TO COMPREHENSION QUESTIONS ON PAGE 27:

1. (Possible response: At first, Lizzie and Harold are best friends, but Lizzie gets upset when Harold also wants to be friends with Douglas. At the end, Lizzie becomes friends with Douglas, too.) INFERENTIAL: SUMMARIZE
2. (Responses will vary.) CRITICAL: EXPRESS PERSONAL OPINIONS
3. (Possible response: that it can be nice to have more than one friend) INFERENTIAL: DETERMINE AUTHOR'S PURPOSE

Response to the Literature

WRITING Children's lists should tell how to be a good friend. Children should number their rules and use complete sentences.

Name ______________________

The Best Friends Club

Answer with complete sentences.

1. How does Lizzie change in the story?

____

____

____

2. If you started a club, what would it be like?

____

____

____

3. What does the author want readers to learn from this story?

____

____

____

RESPONSE TO THE LITERATURE

WRITING On a separate sheet of paper, write a list of rules for being a good friend. Number your rules and write in complete sentences. Share your list with a friend.

Reading Level

Summary

As Amelia Bedelia and her niece Effie Lou help Miss Emma with her household and gardening chores, Amelia Bedelia teaches Effie Lou her befuddled definitions of "dusting" potato bugs, "sewing" seeds, and baking "tea" cakes. Luckily, Miss Emma has a good sense of humor, and Amelia Bedelia's attempts at helping out are well received.

Author Information

Peggy Parish wrote dozens of books for young children, but she is remembered chiefly for her series about a well-meaning housekeeper who continually misunderstands homophones. The Amelia Bedelia books made Peggy Parish one of the most popular authors of books for early readers.

More Books by Peggy Parish

Mind Your Manners

Haunted House

Scruffy

Be Ready at Eight

Good Hunting, Blue Sky

Too Many Rabbits

Amelia Bedelia Helps Out

by Peggy Parish

Introducing the Book

You may wish to ask children the following questions to **build background** and **introduce story vocabulary.**

- What does it mean to weed a garden?
- How would you stake a plant?
- Sometimes gardeners dust a plant for bugs. What does this mean?
- What does it mean to give scraps to an animal?
- What does it mean to sow seed? What is the difference between *sow* and *sew*?

SETTING A PURPOSE Display the book cover and read the title aloud with children. Ask whether they are familiar with the character Amelia Bedelia. Explain that Amelia Bedelia is a humorous character who appears in many books by Peggy Parish. Then have children set a purpose for reading. If they have difficulty setting a purpose, offer this suggestion:

> MODEL **I know that Amelia Bedelia is a funny character in Peggy Parish's books. I'll read to see what funny things she does by helping out.**

Reading Options

DIRECTED READING Use the Monitor Comprehension questions and Guided Reading strategies on pages 29–30 to check children's comprehension. WHOLE CLASS/SMALL GROUP

INDEPENDENT READING Have children read *Amelia Bedelia Helps Out* and complete the comprehension questions on page 31 independently. Encourage them to write their reactions to the story in their Reading Logs. INDIVIDUAL/WHOLE CLASS

Monitor Comprehension

Use these questions to monitor children's comprehension and to evaluate their use of reading strategies.

Pages 4–13

1. **Who is Effie Lou?** (Amelia Bedelia's niece) INFERENTIAL: DRAW CONCLUSIONS
2. **What is the first chore Miss Emma asks Amelia Bedelia to do?** (weed the garden) INFERENTIAL: SEQUENCE
3. **What does Amelia Bedelia think Miss Emma means when she asks her to weed the garden?** (Possible response: She thinks Miss Emma wants more weeds to shade the vegetables in the garden.) INFERENTIAL: DRAW CONCLUSIONS

Guided Reading

FOCUS STRATEGY **REREAD** Tell children that when they are confused by something they read in a story, they should go back and reread that part of the story to find whatever they misunderstood or didn't notice.

Monitor Comprehension

Pages 14–27

4. **How do Amelia Bedelia and Effie stake ("steak") the beans?** (Possible response: They use a saw to cut up pieces of steak and tie them to the plants with string.) INFERENTIAL: SUMMARIZE
5. **What do you think Miss Emma means by "stake the beans"?** (Possible response: Cut wooden stakes, stick each one in the ground by a bean plant, and use string to tie the plant to the stake.) INFERENTIAL: SPECULATE
6. **What does Miss Emma mean when she asks Amelia to dust the potato plants?** (Possible response: She wants Amelia to sprinkle bug powder on the plants.) INFERENTIAL: DRAW CONCLUSIONS

Guided Reading

FOCUS STRATEGY **SEQUENCE EVENTS/SUMMARIZE** Have children think about the order of the story events as they read. Encourage them to think about what has already happened in the story. Then they can read on to find out what happens next.

Monitor Comprehension

Pages 28–40

7. **What is funny about the scraps Amelia and Effie Lou throw to the chickens?** (They are scraps of cloth, not scraps of food.) LITERAL: NOTE DETAILS

8. **What do you think Miss Emma wants when she asks Amelia Bedelia to make a tea cake?** (Possible response: a cake to serve with tea) INFERENTIAL: INTERPRET CHARACTERS' ACTIONS

9. **How does Amelia Bedelia make tea cake?** (Possible response: She mixes tea into the cake batter.) INFERENTIAL: SUMMARIZE

10. **Why does the author have Amelia Bedelia make so many mistakes?** (Possible response: to make the story funny) INFERENTIAL: AUTHOR'S CRAFT

Guided Reading

FOCUS STRATEGY **MAKE AND CONFIRM PREDICTIONS** Give children the opportunity to predict what will happen in the next part of the story. Have them use what they already know about Amelia Bedelia to predict how she will sow grass seeds.

Monitor Comprehension

Pages 41–63

11. **How close did your predictions come to what happened?** (Responses will vary.) INFERENTIAL: CONFIRMING PREDICTIONS

12. **What surprising thing happens when the ladies come over?** (Possible response: They love Amelia's tea cake.) INFERENTIAL: MAIN IDEA

13. **How do you think Miss Emma feels about Amelia Bedelia? How do you know?** (Possible response: Miss Emma must like Amelia because she doesn't get mad at her. She laughs and tells Effie Lou she's lucky to have Amelia Bedelia for an aunt.) METACOGNITIVE: DETERMINE CHARACTERS' EMOTIONS

RETELLING Guidelines for performing a retelling of the story, as well as a rubric for evaluating the retelling, are provided on pages 110–111 of this teacher's guide.

ANSWERS TO COMPREHENSION QUESTIONS ON PAGE 31:

1. (Possible response: Amelia Bedelia misunderstands Miss Emma's directions and makes many funny mistakes in the garden and kitchen.) INFERENTIAL: SUMMARIZE

2. (Responses will vary.) CRITICAL: EXPRESS PERSONAL OPINIONS

3. (Possible response: I would show her what I wanted her to do. I would make sure she understood the meanings of words that sound alike.) CRITICAL: IDENTIFY WITH CHARACTERS

Response to the Literature

WRITING Children should write their own story in which Amelia Bedelia confuses meanings of two or more words. They should use complete sentences.

Name ____________________

Amelia Bedelia Helps Out

Answer with complete sentences.

1. In a sentence or two, summarize this story for someone who hasn't read it.

____

____

____

2. What do you think is the funniest thing Amelia Bedelia does?

____

____

____

3. Suppose you were Miss Emma. How would you help Amelia Bedelia understand your directions?

____

____

____

RESPONSE TO THE LITERATURE

WRITING With your teacher, think of other words that sound alike but mean different things. Then, on a separate sheet of paper, write your own story about Amelia Bedelia. Use two or more of those words in your story. Write in complete sentences.

Reading Level

Summary

Since all his friends are flamingos, Pete thinks he's a flamingo, too. He worries about his color, his lack of feathers, and his four legs. Finally, he meets three other alligators and realizes that there are "flamingos" who look different from the ones he knows.

Author/Illustrator Information

Ellen Stoll Walsh lives in Fairport, New York. She is the author-illustrator of the ALA Notable Books *Hop Jump* and *Mouse Count,* as well as the IRA-CBC Children's Choice *Mouse Paint.*

More Books by Ellen Stoll Walsh

Jack's Tale

Pip's Magic

You Silly Goose

Theodore All Grown Up

Brunus and the New Bear

For Pete's Sake

by Ellen Stoll Walsh

Introducing the Book

You may wish to ask children the following questions to **build background** and **introduce story vocabulary.**

- What does it mean for a fruit to be ripe?
- What do you do when you go wading?
- What kind of animal has feathers?
- What is the difference between friends and strangers?
- How is a flower different from a tree?
- How are you the same as your friends?

SETTING A PURPOSE Display the book cover and read the title aloud with children. Then display some of the pages. Point out Pete the alligator and the flamingos. Remind children that one reason for reading is to be entertained. Have them set a purpose for reading. If they have difficulty setting a purpose, offer this suggestion:

MODEL **I see that this book is about an alligator and some birds called flamingos. I'll read to find out what happens to these animals.**

Reading Options

DIRECTED READING Use the Monitor Comprehension questions and Guided Reading strategies on pages 33–34 to check children's comprehension. WHOLE CLASS/SMALL GROUP

INDEPENDENT READING Have children read *For Pete's Sake* and complete the comprehension questions on page 35 independently. Encourage children to write their reactions to the story in their Reading Logs. INDIVIDUAL/WHOLE CLASS

Monitor Comprehension

Use these questions to monitor children's comprehension and to evaluate their use of reading strategies.

Pages 2–7

1. **What color does Pete want to be?** (pink) LITERAL: NOTE DETAILS
2. **What do the flamingos mean when they tell Pete he is probably not ripe yet?** (Possible response: He is still young; when he is older, he'll change color.) INFERENTIAL: UNDERSTAND FIGURATIVE LANGUAGE
3. **Why does Pete think everyone is pink?** (Possible response: He only sees flamingos and they are pink.) INFERENTIAL: SPECULATE

Guided Reading

FOCUS STRATEGY **CREATE MENTAL IMAGES** Tell children that sometimes they can understand a story better if they picture in their minds what is happening. Have children picture Pete ripening like an apple. What do they see?

Monitor Comprehension

Pages 8–19

4. **How else is Pete different from the flamingos?** (Possible response: He has four feet and they have two; he doesn't have any feathers and they do.) INFERENTIAL: COMPARE AND CONTRAST
5. **How do you know that the flamingos like Pete?** (Possible response: They tell him he's lucky to have four feet; they tell him the best feathers take the longest to grow; they play with him.) METACOGNITIVE: DRAW CONCLUSIONS
6. **Why do you think Pete wants to look like a flamingo?** (Possible response: He wants to fit in; he wants to look like everyone else.) INFERENTIAL: DETERMINE CHARACTERS' EMOTIONS

Guided Reading

FOCUS STRATEGY **USE PICTURE CLUES TO CONFIRM MEANING** Ask children how the picture on page 12 helps them make sure they understand the word *wading* on page 11. Remind children that the pictures in a story can help them make sure the words they read were right.

Monitor Comprehension

Pages 20–25

7. **How do you think Pete feels as he walks home?** (Possible responses: lonely, sad, different) INFERENTIAL: DETERMINE CHARACTERS' EMOTIONS
8. **Why can't the flamingos cheer Pete up anymore?** (Possible response: Pete knows he will never be like them; he will never have two long legs or feathers.) INFERENTIAL: SYNTHESIZE
9. **What do you think will happen next?** (Responses will vary.) INFERENTIAL: MAKE PREDICTIONS

Guided Reading

FOCUS STRATEGY **MAKE AND CONFIRM PREDICTIONS** Have children use what they know about Pete and the story so far to predict what will happen next.

Monitor Comprehension

Pages 26–29

10. **How did your predictions compare to what happened?** (Responses will vary.) INFERENTIAL: CONFIRM PREDICTIONS
11. **What does Pete mean when he says, "I'm different but the same"?** (Possible response: He is different from the flamingos but the same as the alligators, which he thinks are a different kind of flamingo.) INFERENTIAL: DRAW CONCLUSIONS
12. **Why do you think the author chose to end the story this way?** (Possible response: to show that Pete can feel good about being different) CRITICAL: RECOGNIZE AUTHOR'S PURPOSE

RETELLING Guidelines for performing a retelling of the story, as well as a rubric for evaluating the retelling, are provided on pages 110–111 of this teacher's guide.

ANSWERS TO COMPREHENSION QUESTIONS ON PAGE 35:

1. (Possible response: At first, he is unhappy and wants to be like his friends, the flamingos. At the end, he is happy to find out that he is supposed to be different, when he finds others just like himself.) INFERENTIAL: SUMMARIZE
2. (Responses will vary.) CRITICAL: PERSONAL RESPONSE
3. (Possible responses: It is okay to be different; you can be different from others and still be their friends.) CRITICAL: INTERPRET THEME

Response to the Literature

WRITING Children should write a paragraph explaining why *For Pete's Sake* would or would not be a good book to read aloud to younger children. Children should use complete sentences.

Name ______________________________

For Pete's Sake

Write answers to these questions in complete sentences.

1. How do Pete's feelings about being different change?

____

____

____

2. If you were a flamingo, would you be friends with Pete? Why or why not?

____

____

____

3. What does this book tell you about being different?

____

____

____

RESPONSE TO THE LITERATURE

WRITING Would *For Pete's Sake* be a good book to read aloud to younger children? On a separate sheet of paper, write a paragraph telling your reasons. Use complete sentences.

Reading Level

Summary

When Simon gets an invisible dragon friend named Dexter, he starts leaving his brother, Alex, out of every activity. Feeling lonely, Alex invents his own imaginary friend, a camel named Calvin. Soon, Calvin and Dexter are having all the fun, and the brothers feel left out. Finally, Dexter and Calvin "move to Boston," leaving the brothers to work out their differences and become best friends again.

Author Information

James Howe has written a number of popular books for children, including the prequel to this book, *There's a Monster Under My Bed.* He lives in Hastings-on-Hudson, New York, with his wife and daughter.

More Books by James Howe

Bunnicula: A Rabbit-Tale of Mystery (with Deborah Howe)

I Wish I Were a Butterfly

The Day the Teacher Went Bananas

Horace and Morris but Mostly Dolores

Harold and Chester in Hot Fudge

There's a Dragon in My Sleeping Bag

by James Howe

Introducing the Book

You may wish to ask children the following questions to **build background** and **introduce story vocabulary.**

- What is a dragon like?
- What does a camel look like?
- What does it mean to notice something?
- What does it mean to have company for dinner?

SETTING A PURPOSE Display the book cover and read the title aloud with children. Ask them what this story might be about. Then remind children that one purpose for reading is to be entertained. Have them set a purpose for reading. If they have difficulty setting a purpose, offer this suggestion:

> MODEL **I see that this book is about a dragon and two boys. The dragon is in one boy's sleeping bag. I'll read to find out what happens to the dragon.**

Reading Options

DIRECTED READING Use the Monitor Comprehension questions and Guided Reading strategies on pages 37–38 to check children's comprehension. WHOLE CLASS/SMALL GROUP

INDEPENDENT READING Have children read *There's a Dragon in My Sleeping Bag* and complete the comprehension questions on page 39 independently. Encourage children to write their reactions to the story in their Reading Logs. INDIVIDUAL/WHOLE CLASS

Monitor Comprehension

Use these questions to monitor students' comprehension and to evaluate their use of reading strategies.

Pages 1–7

1. **Who is telling the story? What is his problem?** (Possible response: A boy; his brother, Simon, keeps telling him there is a dragon.) INFERENTIAL: MAIN IDEA
2. **Is the dragon real? How do you know?** (Possible response: No. The boy can't see it.) INFERENTIAL: DRAW CONCLUSIONS
3. **How do you think the boy feels about the dragon? How can you tell?** (Possible response: He doesn't like it. I can tell because he doesn't look happy that the dragon has taken his place.) INFERENTIAL: DETERMINE CHARACTERS' EMOTIONS

Guided Reading

FOCUS STRATEGY **LOOK AT WORD BITS AND PARTS** Remind children that one way to figure out an unfamiliar word is to look for smaller words they know inside the longer word. Children may apply this strategy to reading words such as *somwhere*, *breakfast*, and *seesaw*.

Monitor Comprehension

Pages 8–13

4. **Who does the boy play with?** (Calvin, the camel) LITERAL: NOTE DETAILS
5. **Is Calvin a real camel? How do you know?** (Possible response: No. Simon can't see Calvin.) INFERENTIAL: DRAW CONCLUSIONS
6. **What do you think will happen next?** (Responses will vary.) INFERENTIAL: MAKE PREDICTIONS

Guided Reading

FOCUS STRATEGY **SEQUENCE EVENTS/SUMMARIZE** Tell children to think about the order of story events as they read. Encourage them to think about what has already happened in the story. Then they can read on to find out what happens next.

Monitor Comprehension

Pages 14–20

7. **How did your predictions compare to what happened?** (Responses will vary.) INFERENTIAL: CONFIRM PREDICTIONS

8. **Why does Simon say, "Dexter was more fun before Calvin got here"?** (Possible response: Now Dexter plays with Calvin, and the boys are left out.) INFERENTIAL: DRAW CONCLUSIONS

9. **Why can't the boys sleep in the same room anymore?** (Possible response: Calvin and Dexter are in the boys' sleeping bags, so the boys have to sleep in separate rooms.) INFERENTIAL: CAUSE-EFFECT

Guided Reading

FOCUS STRATEGY **MAKE AND CONFIRM PREDICTIONS** Give children an opportunity to predict what will happen in the next part of the story.

Monitor Comprehension

Pages 21–27

10. **How close did your predictions come to what happened?** (Responses will vary.) INFERENTIAL: CONFIRM PREDICTIONS

11. **What happens to Dexter and Calvin?** (They move to Boston together.) LITERAL: NOTE DETAILS

12. **What lesson do the brothers learn in this story?** (Possible response: A real, live brother is better than any pretend friend.) INFERENTIAL: DETERMINE THEME

RETELLING Guidelines for performing a retelling of the story, as well as a rubric for evaluating the retelling, are provided on pages 110–111 of this teacher's guide.

ANSWERS TO COMPREHENSION QUESTIONS ON PAGE 39:

1. (Possible response: Simon has an imaginary friend, named Dexter. His brother feels left out, so he makes an imaginary friend, named Calvin. Calvin and Dexter become friends and leave the boys out. The boys pretend that Dexter and Calvin move to Boston together. This way, the brothers can do things together again.) INFERENTIAL: SUMMARIZE
2. (Responses will vary.) CRITICAL: PERSONAL RESPONSE
3. (Possible response: The pretend friends could disappear; real, live friends would not be able to disappear so easily from the boys' lives.) INFERENTIAL: DETERMINE AUTHOR'S PURPOSE

Response to the Literature

WRITING Children's poems about friendship should include some ideas from the story.

Name ______________________________

There's a Dragon in My Sleeping Bag

Write answers to these questions in complete sentences.

1. What are the main events in this story?

____

____

____

2. Do you agree with Simon that being brothers is better than being best friends? Why or why not?

____

____

____

3. Why did the author give the boys pretend friends instead of real, live friends?

____

____

____

RESPONSE TO THE LITERATURE

WRITING On a separate sheet of paper, write a poem about friendship. Use some of the ideas in the story. Your poem does not have to rhyme.

Reading Level

Summary

Rooster gets his beak dirty on the way to his uncle's wedding. He asks the grass, a lamb, a dog, a stick, a fire, and some water for help, but all refuse. Finally, he asks his friend, the sun. A threat from the sun causes everyone along the chain to offer the help the rooster needs.

Author Information

An accomplished translator of children's books from English to Spanish, **Alma Flor Ada** was born in Cuba and has lived in Spain, Peru, and the United States. Her original fiction often introduces children to Central and South American landscapes and cultures.

More Books by Alma Flor Ada

The Gold Coin

Gathering the Sun: An Alphabet in Spanish and English

Dear Peter Rabbit

Jordi's Star

The Rooster Who Went to His Uncle's Wedding

by Alma Flor Ada

Introducing the Book

You may wish to ask children the following questions to **build background** and **introduce story vocabulary.**

- What does something that is shining look like?
- What is a kernel of corn?
- What does grazing mean? What kinds of animals graze?
- If someone strutted into a room, what would he or she be doing?
- Why would people sit around a campfire?
- What is a brook? Where would you find one?

SETTING A PURPOSE Display the book cover and display the first few illustrations. Remind children that one purpose for reading is to be entertained. Have them set a purpose for reading. If children have difficulty setting a purpose, offer this suggestion:

> MODEL **This rooster looks like a funny character. I'll read to find out what funny things happen when he goes to his uncle's wedding.**

Reading Options

DIRECTED READING Use the Monitor Comprehension questions and Guided Reading strategies on pages 41–42 to check children's comprehension. WHOLE CLASS/SMALL GROUP

INDEPENDENT READING Have children read *The Rooster Who Went to His Uncle's Wedding* and complete the comprehension questions on page 43 independently. Encourage children to write their reactions to the story in their Reading Logs. INDIVIDUAL/WHOLE CLASS

Monitor Comprehension

Use these questions to monitor children's comprehension and to evaluate their use of reading strategies.

Pages 2–9

1. **What is the rooster thinking about as he walks down the road?** (all the wonderful things at the wedding banquet) LITERAL: NOTE DETAILS
2. **Why does the rooster stop to think before he eats the kernel of corn?** (Possible response: He is hungry, but the kernel is lying in a mud puddle and he doesn't want his beak to be muddy at the wedding.) INFERENTIAL: CAUSE-EFFECT
3. **What happens when the rooster gobbles the kernel?** (Possible response: He gets a beak full of mud.) LITERAL: CAUSE-EFFECT

Guided Reading

FOCUS STRATEGY **SELF-CORRECT** Remind children that sometimes they may notice that the letters in a word do not match the way they have read it. Have children correct themselves when this happens by looking carefully at the word and rereading it.

Monitor Comprehension

Pages 10–17

4. **Who does the rooster ask first for help?** (the grass) LITERAL: NOTE DETAILS
5. **What does the rooster ask the next three characters to do?** (He asks the lamb to eat the grass, the dog to bite the lamb, and the stick to hit the dog.) LITERAL: SEQUENCE
6. **What do you think will happen next? Why?** (Possible response: The rooster will look for something that will make the stick hit the dog; because that is the pattern of the story.) INFERENTIAL: TEXT STRUCTURE/MAKE PREDICTIONS

Guided Reading

FOCUS STRATEGY **SEQUENCE EVENTS/SUMMARIZE** Tell children to think about the order of story events as they read. Encourage them to think about what has already happened in the story and to look for a pattern in the events. Then they can read on to find out what happens next.

Monitor Comprehension

Pages 18–23

7. **What does the rooster ask the campfire and the brook to do?** (He asks the fire to burn the stick and the brook to put out the fire.) LITERAL: NOTE DETAILS
8. **Why do you think all of the characters refuse to help the rooster?** (Responses will vary.) CRITICAL: EXPRESS PERSONAL OPINIONS
9. **Why does the sun want to help the rooster?** (Possible response: because the rooster sings to the sun every morning) INFERENTIAL: DRAW CONCLUSIONS

Guided Reading

FOCUS STRATEGY **MAKE AND CONFIRM PREDICTIONS** Give children the opportunity to predict what will happen in the next part of the story.

Monitor Comprehension

Pages 24–30

10. **How close were your predictions to what happened?** (Responses will vary.) INFERENTIAL: CONFIRM PREDICTIONS
11. **Why do all the characters suddenly change their minds?** (Possible response: They are all afraid of being hurt by someone else if they don't do something.) INFERENTIAL: CAUSE-EFFECT
12. **How does the rooster feel when he goes to the wedding?** (Possible response: happy) INFERENTIAL: DRAW CONCLUSIONS

RETELLING Guidelines for performing a retelling of the story, as well as a rubric for evaluating the retelling, are provided on pages 110–111 of this teacher's guide.

ANSWERS TO COMPREHENSION QUESTIONS ON PAGE 43:

1. (Possible response: He gets the sun to dry up the brook if it doesn't put out the campfire if it doesn't burn the stick if it doesn't hit the dog if it doesn't bite the lamb if it doesn't eat the grass if it doesn't clean the rooster's beak.) INFERENTIAL: SUMMARIZE
2. (Responses will vary.) CRITICAL: EXPRESS PERSONAL OPINIONS
3. (Possible response: Repeating parts of the story makes the story easy to read and remember.) CRITICAL: RECOGNIZE AUTHOR'S PURPOSE

Response to the Literature

WRITING Children should write a tale based on a pattern like that in *The Rooster Who Went to His Uncle's Wedding*. Children should use complete sentences and a paragraph format.

Name ______________________________

The Rooster Who Went to His Uncle's Wedding

Answer with complete sentences.

1. How does the rooster get the grass to clean his beak?

____

____

____

2. Do you think the rooster is a character you would like to know? Explain your answer.

____

____

____

3. Why does the author repeat parts of this story?

____

____

____

RESPONSE TO THE LITERATURE

WRITING Many folktales are written in a pattern like the pattern in *The Rooster Who Went to His Uncle's Wedding.* On separate sheets of paper, write your own tale by using a pattern. Start with a character who has a problem to solve. Tell how the character solves the problem. Use complete sentences and a paragraph format.

Reading Level

Summary

Lars the polar bear helps Hugo the hare out of a hole. On the way home, Lars teases Hugo for being afraid of a steep slope, a car, and a research station but hides his own fears. Then, while Lars is exploring the station, he falls through a hole in the roof. A man enters the station, and Hugo summons the courage to distract him so Lars can escape. Now Lars knows his friend is not a "scaredy-hare."

Author/Illustrator Information

Hans de Beer was born and lives in Holland. As a student, he would draw whenever he was bored in school. Eventually, he entered an art school and went on to become a prize-winning illustrator of picture books. De Beer's first book, *Little Polar Bear,* has been published in 18 languages.

More Books by Hans de Beer

Little Polar Bear Finds a Friend

Little Polar Bear, Take Me Home

Books Illustrated by Hans de Beer

The Big Squirrel and the Little Rhinoceros

Leave It to the Molesons

More from the Molesons

Little Bobo

Little Polar Bear and the Brave Little Hare

by Hans de Beer

Introducing the Book

You may wish to ask children the following questions to **build background** and **introduce story vocabulary.**

- What does a polar bear look like?
- What is a hare?
- What does it mean to say someone's heart thumped? What might make someone's heart thump?
- Do you remember a time when you shivered? Why did you shiver?
- What does it mean to have courage?
- What does it mean to be embarrassed?
- What might a brave person do to show he or she is brave?

SETTING A PURPOSE Display the book cover and a few of the illustrations. Remind children that one purpose for reading is to be entertained. Have children set a purpose for reading. If they have difficulty setting a purpose, offer this suggestion:

> MODEL **I see that this story is about a polar bear and a rabbit—a hare. I'll read to find out what makes the hare brave.**

Reading Options

DIRECTED READING Use the Monitor Comprehension questions and Guided Reading strategies on pages 45–46 to check children's comprehension. WHOLE CLASS/SMALL GROUP

INDEPENDENT READING Have children read *The Polar Bear and the Brave Little Hare* and complete the comprehension questions on page 47 independently. Encourage children to write their reactions to the story in their Reading Logs. INDIVIDUAL/WHOLE CLASS

Monitor Comprehension

Use these questions to monitor children's comprehension and evaluate their use of reading strategies.

Pages 6–15

1. **What is it like at the North Pole where Lars lives?** (Possible responses: there are hills, ice, snow; it is near the sea; it is very quiet; sometimes it is windy) INFERENTIAL: NOTE DETAILS
2. **How does Lars help the hare get out of the deep hole?** (He kicks down a pile of snow so the little hare can climb up on the snow and out of the hole.) LITERAL: CAUSE-EFFECT
3. **Why do you think Lars wants to show Hugo that he is a brave polar bear?** (Possible responses: He doesn't want Hugo to be afraid; he wants to show off.) CRITICAL: INTERPRET CHARACTERS' MOTIVATIONS

Guided Reading

FOCUS STRATEGY **CREATE MENTAL IMAGES** Point out to children that sometimes they can understand a story better when they picture in their minds what is happening. Suggest that they imagine Lars and Hugo building a pile of snow and think about how this would protect them against the wind.

Monitor Comprehension

Pages 16–23

4. **Why do you think polar bears like Lars's father could find food at the research station?** (Possible response: People working at the research station may throw food away, and bears and other animals find and eat it.) INFERENTIAL: SPECULATE
5. **Why does Lars call Hugo a scaredy-hare?** (Possible response: Hugo won't slide down a steep slope, he hides from the car, and he doesn't like the station.) INFERENTIAL: CAUSE-EFFECT
6. **What do you think will happen next?** (Responses will vary.) INFERENTIAL: MAKE PREDICTIONS

Guided Reading

FOCUS STRATEGY **SEQUENCE EVENTS/SUMMARIZE** Tell children to think about the order of story events as they read. Encourage them to think about what has already happened in the story. Then they can read on to find out what happens next.

Monitor Comprehension

Pages 24–33

7. **How does Lars get into the research station?** (Possible response: He climbs up on the roof and falls into the station.) INFERENTIAL: SUMMARIZE
8. **Why does Hugo go up on the roof?** (Possible response: to kick snow through the hole and get the man's attention so he won't find Lars) INFERENTIAL: CAUSE-EFFECT
9. **How do you know that Lars is safe?** (The man leaves to get a ladder; he does not see Lars.) METACOGNITIVE: NOTE DETAILS

Guided Reading

FOCUS STRATEGY **MAKE PREDICTIONS** Give children the opportunity to predict what will happen in the next part of the story.

Monitor Comprehension

Pages 34–43

10. **How close did your predictions come to what happens?** (Responses will vary.) INFERENTIAL: CONFIRM PREDICTIONS
11. **How does Lars get out of the station?** (The man leaves the door open so Lars gets out.) INFERENTIAL: DRAW CONCLUSIONS
12. **What is the message of the story?** (Possible response: You can be brave when you have to be, even if you're scared.) INFERENTIAL: DETERMINE AUTHOR'S PURPOSE

RETELLING Guidelines for performing a retelling of the story, as well as a rubric for evaluating the retelling, are provided on pages 110–111 of this teacher's guide.

ANSWERS TO COMPREHENSION QUESTIONS ON PAGE 47:

1. (Possible response: At first, Lars pretends to be brave about everything, and he calls Hugo a scaredy-hare. After he falls into the station, he thinks Hugo is brave to rescue him and he stops calling him a scaredy-hare.) INFERENTIAL: SUMMARIZE
2. (Responses will vary.) CRITICAL: EXPRESS PERSONAL OPINIONS
3. (Possible response: Hugo risks his life to save Lars, and that is really brave.) CRITICAL: LITERARY ANALYSIS

Response to the Literature

WRITING Children's stories should tell how a timid animal character helps a brave one. Children should use complete sentences.

Name ______________________________

Little Polar Bear and the Brave Little Hare

Answer with complete sentences.

1. Think about Lars before and after he falls into the research station. How does he change?

____

____

____

2. Do you think Lars and Hugo will have more adventures? Explain your answer.

____

____

____

3. Hugo says, "I was not brave." Do you agree? Explain your answer.

____

____

____

RESPONSE TO THE LITERATURE

WRITING Write your own story in which a brave animal character is helped by a scared one. Use complete sentences.

Reading Level

Summary

Alistair, a sensible and responsible boy, sets out for the library to return books. Suddenly, a spaceship appears and two creatures called Goots whisk Alistair off into outer space. After the Goots make a wrong turn, Alistair rereads his books and shows his library card to the aliens, but when the trip threatens to cost him a library fine, Alistair takes over the ship. He lands with time to spare—at the South Pole!

Author and Illustrator Information

Marilyn Sadler has said, "I am attracted to the funniest things in life and feel most comfortable when I tell my stories from a humorous point of view." Her stories are illustrated by her husband, **Roger Bollen,** a professional cartoonist. Together they have created more than twenty books for young readers. Their popular characters include Alistair Grittle and P. J. Funnybunny.

More Books by Marilyn Sadler

Alistair and the Alien Invasion

Alistair Underwater

Alistair's Elephant

It's Not Easy Being a Bunny

The Parakeet Girl

Zenon: Girl of the 21st Century

Alistair in Outer Space

by Marilyn Sadler

Introducing the Book

You may wish to ask children the following questions to **build background** and **introduce story vocabulary.**

- What is someone like who is sensible?
- What might happen on an unusual day?
- If something is whisked away, what happened to it?
- What kind of adventure would you like to have?
- Why is it a good idea to ask for directions?
- What is a shortcut?

SETTING A PURPOSE Display the book cover, read aloud the title, and point out Alistair. Remind children that one purpose for reading is to be entertained. Have children set a purpose for reading. If they have difficulty setting a purpose, offer this suggestion:

> MODEL **I'll read this book to find out how Alistair gets into outer space, and what happens to him there.**

Reading Options

DIRECTED READING Use the Monitor Comprehension questions and Guided Reading strategies on pages 49–50 to check children's comprehension. WHOLE CLASS/SMALL GROUP

INDEPENDENT READING Have children read *Alistair in Outer Space* and complete the comprehension questions on page 51 independently. Encourage children to write their reactions to the story in their Reading Logs. INDIVIDUAL/WHOLE CLASS

Monitor Comprehension

Use these questions to monitor children's comprehension and evaluate their use of reading strategies.

Pages 2–9

1. **What does Alistair do that shows he is sensible?** (Possible responses: He makes lists, he is on time, he puts up his clothes, and he takes his library books back on time.) INFERENTIAL: DETERMINE CHARACTERS' TRAITS
2. **Why do you think the school's clock is set by Alistair's watch?** (Possible response: Alistair's watch is always correct.) INFERENTIAL: DRAW CONCLUSIONS
3. **What do you think will happen next?** (Responses will vary.) INFERENTIAL: MAKE PREDICTIONS

Guided Reading

FOCUS STRATEGY **LOOK AT WORD BITS AND PARTS** Remind children that one way to figure out an unfamiliar word is to look for smaller words they know inside the longer word. Children may apply this strategy to reading words such as *especially*, *returning*, and *happening*.

Monitor Comprehension

Pages 10–19

4. **How did your prediction compare to what happens?** (Responses will vary.) INFERENTIAL: CONFIRM PREDICTIONS
5. **Why doesn't Alistair want to go with the Goots?** (He wants to return his library books on time.) LITERAL: NOTE DETAILS
6. **How does Alistair fall out of the spaceship?** (He opens the wrong door while he is looking for a place to wash his hands.) INFERENTIAL: CAUSE-EFFECT

Guided Reading

FOCUS STRATEGY **SELF-CORRECT** Tell children that sometimes when they read a word and it doesn't make sense, they might notice that the letters in the word do not match the way they have read it. Have children correct themselves when this happens by looking carefully at the word and rereading it.

Monitor Comprehension

Pages 20–27

7. **How does Alistair feel about being in outer space?** (Possible response: He doesn't seem to care about anything but returning his library books on time.) INFERENTIAL: DETERMINE CHARACTERS' EMOTIONS

8. **Why does Alistair get upset with the Goots?** (Possible response: He wants to get home before he has to pay a fine on his library books.) INFERENTIAL: DETERMINE CHARACTERS' EMOTIONS

9. **Do you think this book is funny? Why or why not?** (Possible response: Yes; the pictures, the characters, and Alistair's worry about the library books make it funny.) INFERENTIAL: AUTHOR'S CRAFT

Guided Reading

FOCUS STRATEGY **MAKE PREDICTIONS** Give children the opportunity to predict what will happen in the next part of the story.

Monitor Comprehension

Pages 28–37

10. **Why does Alistair fly the spaceship?** (He doesn't think the Goots will be able to find Earth.) LITERAL: CAUSE-EFFECT

11. **Why is Alistair relieved when the spaceship lands?** (He thinks there is still time to get to the library.) LITERAL: CAUSE-EFFECT

12. **What is the surprise ending?** (Possible response: Alistair has landed at the South Pole—nowhere near his library.) INFERENTIAL: AUTHOR'S CRAFT

RETELLING Guidelines for performing a retelling of the story, as well as a rubric for evaluating the retelling, are provided on pages 110–111 of this teacher's guide.

ANSWERS TO COMPREHENSION QUESTIONS ON PAGE 51:

1. (Possible response: Alistair is taken into outer space. All he can think about is getting to the library on time. He finally lands on Earth at the South Pole.) INFERENTIAL: SUMMARIZE

2. (Responses will vary.) CRITICAL: EXPRESS PERSONAL OPINIONS

3. (Possible response: He will probably figure out a way to get home from the South Pole.) CRITICAL: SPECULATE

Response to the Literature

WRITING Children's stories should tell how Alistair gets to the library from the South Pole. They should not change Alistair's character too much. Stories should contain complete sentences.

Name ______________________________

Alistair in Outer Space

Answer with complete sentences.

1. What are the most important events in this story?

____

____

____

2. How would you feel if you had an adventure like Alistair's?

____

____

____

____

3. What do you think Alistair will do when he realizes he is at the South Pole?

____

____

____

RESPONSE TO THE LITERATURE

WRITING Write a story about how Alistair finally gets to the library from the South Pole. In your story, make sure Alistair is still very sensible. Use complete sentences in your final draft.

Reading Level

Summary

Animals in a classroom take turns explaining the family trees they have made for a class project. One student comes from a traditional family, one is adopted, some are from blended families, and so on. Each family tree is shown in its entirety, and terms for family members are included in a glossary.

Author/Illustrator Information

Loreen Leedy lives in Winter Park, Florida. She has written and illustrated a number of books for children, including *Postcards from Pluto: A Tour of the Solar System.*

More Books by Loreen Leedy

The Edible Pyramid: Good Eating Every Day

Postcards from Pluto: A Tour of the Solar System

Messages in the Mailbox: How to Write a Letter

The Furry News: How to Make a Newspaper

Mission—Addition

Fraction Action

Measuring Penny

The Great Trash Bash

How Humans Make Friends

Blast Off to Earth

The Monster Money Book

Pingo the Plaid Panda

Who's Who in My Family?

by Loreen Leedy

Introducing the Book

You may wish to ask children the following questions to **build background** and **introduce story vocabulary.**

- What is a family tree? Have you ever drawn a family tree?
- What is a hobby? What are your hobbies?
- How are parents, grandparents, and great-grandparents related to you?
- How are brothers and sisters related?
- What are aunts? What is an uncle?
- What is a spouse?
- How are cousins related?
- Who would your great-aunts and great-uncles be? Do you have any?
- What does it mean to be adopted into a family?
- How does a stepparent, stepbrother, or stepsister come into a family?

SETTING A PURPOSE Display the book and show children a picture of a family tree. Remind them that one purpose for reading is to learn. Have children set a purpose for reading. If they have difficulty setting a purpose, offer this suggestion:

> MODEL **This book is about family trees. I'll read to learn more about family trees and to find out who's who in a family.**

Reading Options

DIRECTED READING Use the questions on pages 57–58 to check children's comprehension. WHOLE CLASS/SMALL GROUP

INDEPENDENT READING Have children read *Who's Who in My Family?* and complete the Comprehension Questions independently. Encourage children to write their reactions to the story in their Reading Notebooks. INDIVIDUAL/WHOLE CLASS

Monitor Comprehension

Use these questions to monitor children's comprehension and evaluate their use of reading strategies.

Pages 1–9

1. **Where is this story taking place?** (school [Woodlands Elementary])
   LITERAL: NOTE DETAILS/PICTURE CLUES
2. **What have students been doing?** (making diagrams called family trees)
   INFERENTIAL: DRAW CONCLUSIONS
3. **What is Sandy going to tell readers?** (who is who in her family tree)
   INFERENTIAL: TEXT STRUCTURE
4. **How does Sandy's family compare to yours?** (Responses will vary.)
   INFERENTIAL: MAKE COMPARISONS

Guided Reading

FOCUS STRATEGY **USE PICTURE CLUES TO CONFIRM MEANING** Have children look closely at the picture of Sandy on page 4 and locate that section in the complete family tree on page 3. On page 3, have them identify Sandy (Me!) and her immediate family. Emphasize that readers must use the illustrations to understand the information in this book.

Monitor Comprehension

Pages 10–17

5. **Who are Sandy's aunts and uncles?** (her parents' brothers and sisters, and the wives and husbands of her parents' brothers and sisters) INFERENTIAL: IMPORTANT DETAILS
6. **How do people become part of Sandy's family tree?** (They are born or marry into the family.) INFERENTIAL: GENERALIZE
7. **Which grandparent had the most siblings (brothers and sisters)?** (Pop-pop: he had one of each; the others had only one sibling each.) INFERENTIAL: COMPARE AND CONTRAST

Guided Reading

FOCUS STRATEGY **REREAD** Ask children how they found the answers to the questions. Point out that going back to reread or look again at illustrations is an important strategy for finding and confirming information.

Monitor Comprehension

Pages 18–25

8. **How did the raccoon come into his family?** (adoption) LITERAL: NOTE DETAILS
9. **As the rabbit and skunk family trees show, what is another way people can come into families?** (When a parent remarries, two families are joined.) INFERENTIAL: GENERALIZE
10. **What is the difference between stepsisters and half sisters?** (Stepsisters were born to separate sets of parents; half sisters share one parent by birth but not the other.) INFERENTIAL: COMPARE AND CONTRAST

Guided Reading

FOCUS STRATEGY **MAKE PREDICTIONS** Give children the opportunity to predict what else the book might tell about family trees.

Monitor Comprehension

Pages 26–28

11. **What ancestor do second cousins share?** (a great-grandparent) INFERENTIAL: DRAW CONCLUSIONS
12. **Why does the author say, "It's easier just to call them all cousins"?** (It's difficult to show and harder to explain how cousins can be related.) INFERENTIAL: CAUSE-EFFECT
13. **Why does the author put a list of terms and definitions on the last page?** (Possible response: Readers can use the list to review what they've learned; they can also use alphabetical order to look up a term they've forgotten the meaning of.) INFERENTIAL: DETERMINE AUTHOR'S PURPOSE

RETELLING Guidelines for performing a retelling of the story, as well as a rubric for evaluating the retelling, are provided on pages 116–117 of this teacher's guide.

ANSWERS TO COMPREHENSION QUESTIONS ON PAGE 55:

1. (Possible response: Children are in the bottom row; parents, aunts, and uncles are in the next row; grandparents and great-aunts and -uncles are next; great-grandparents are in the top row.) INFERENTIAL: SUMMARIZE
2. (Possible response: At first I thought family trees were confusing, but after reading the book I'd like to try making one.) CRITICAL: PERSONAL RESPONSE
3. (Possible response: It is helpful to show how people are related because that can be hard to understand in words.) CRITICAL: MAIN IDEA

Response to the Literature

WRITING ACTIVITY Children should make their own family trees, using the model at the beginning of *Who's Who in My Family?* as a guide. Where they don't know a name, they should just indicate the relation—for example, "Uncle."

Name ____________________

Who's Who in My Family?

Answer the questions in complete sentences.

1. Row by row, how is a family tree organized?

____

____

____

2. Some people think family trees are interesting. Other people think they are confusing. What do you think? Explain your answer.

____

____

____

3. Why is it helpful to draw a family tree?

____

____

____

RESPONSE TO THE LITERATURE

WRITING ACTIVITY Draw and label your own family tree. Use the diagram in the beginning of *Who's Who in My Family?* as a guide. Change the diagram to show your family. If you aren't sure about someone's name, just write the relation to you. For example, if you don't know the name of your father's brother, just write "Uncle."

Reading Level

Summary

The author shows flowers on trees and shrubs, in gardens and in meadows; flowers with many petals and flowers with none; flowers that smell nice and flowers that smell terrible. The author then examines the fact that flowers produce fruits and fruits contain seeds that grow into new plants. He illustrates the cycle of plant life that leads from seed to flower to fruit.

About the Author/ Photographer

Jerome Wexler is a nature photographer who has written on a variety of nature topics for children—from frogs to hamsters, and from pussy willows to Venus flytraps.

More Books by Jerome Wexler

Flytraps
Everyday Mysteries
Queen Anne's Lace
Popcorn Plants
Sundew Stranglers: Plants That Eat Insects
Jack-in-the-Pulpit

Flowers, Fruits, Seeds

by Jerome Wexler

Introducing the Book

You may wish to ask children the following questions to **build background** and **introduce story vocabulary**.

- What are your favorite flowers?
- Can you think of any flowers that do not have petals?
- What fruits do you most like to eat? Which do you like the least?
- What fruits taste good raw?
- What kind of seeds would you like to plant?
- If you are not sure if something is poisonous, how can you find out?

SETTING A PURPOSE Display the book cover, and show children some of the photographs. Tell children that one purpose for reading is to be informed. Have them set a purpose for reading *Flowers, Fruits, Seeds.* If children have difficulty setting a purpose, offer this suggestion:

MODEL **The pictures show many types of flowers, fruits, and seeds. I'll read to find out some interesting facts about them.**

Reading Options

DIRECTED READING Use the Monitor Comprehension questions and Guided Reading strategies on pages 57–58 to check children's comprehension. WHOLE CLASS/SMALL GROUP

INDEPENDENT READING Have children read *Flowers, Fruits, Seeds* and complete the comprehension questions on page 59 independently. Encourage children to write their reactions to the story in their Reading Logs. INDIVIDUAL/WHOLE CLASS

Monitor Comprehension

Use these questions to monitor children's comprehension and evaluate their use of reading strategies.

Pages 2–11

1. **What are some plants that have flowers?** (Possible responses: trees, shrubs, bushes, vines, tomato plants, grasses, weeds, house plants) INFERENTIAL: SUMMARIZE
2. **What do the words in small type near each photograph tell you?** (the name of each plant or flower) INFERENTIAL: TEXT STRUCTURE
3. **What is the main purpose of a flower?** (to produce fruits that contain seeds) LITERAL: NOTE DETAILS

Guided Reading

FOCUS STRATEGY **REREAD** Ask children what they should do if they are confused about something they read. (They should reread that part.) Point out that by rereading, children may notice important details that will help them better understand what they are reading.

Monitor Comprehension

Pages 12–17

4. **Why does the photograph on page 11 show a person's fingers holding a flower?** (Possible response: to show how small the flower is) INFERENTIAL: COMPARE AND CONTRAST
5. **How big is the Carron flower on page 12?** (Possible response: about one foot wide) INFERENTIAL: USE PICTURE CLUES
6. **What kind of flower smells bad?** (the skunk cabbage flower) LITERAL: NOTE DETAILS

Guided Reading

FOCUS STRATEGY **USE PICTURE CLUES TO CONFIRM MEANING** Remind children that the pictures in a book can sometimes help them make sure the words they read were right. Have children use this strategy as they read the words *petals* on page 13 and *colorful* on page 14.

Monitor Comprehension

Pages 18–23

7. **What new fact did you learn about fruits?** (Responses will vary.)
   INFERENTIAL: SYNTHESIZE

8. **Which fruit is poisonous?** (Possible response: Jack-in-the-Pulpit fruit)
   INFERENTIAL: USE PICTURE CLUES

9. **What is the main purpose of fruit?** (to protect the seeds inside it)
   LITERAL: NOTE DETAILS

Guided Reading

FOCUS STRATEGY **SEQUENCE EVENTS/SUMMARIZE** Give children the opportunity to sequence and summarize the information they have read so far.

Monitor Comprehension

Pages 24–30

10. **Why do you think seeds come in different sizes and shapes?** (Responses will vary.) INFERENTIAL: SPECULATE

11. **What are seeds for?** (Seeds are for growing new plants.) LITERAL: NOTE DETAILS

RETELLING Guidelines for performing a retelling of the story, as well as a rubric for evaluating the retelling, are provided on pages 110–111 of this teacher's guide.

ANSWERS TO COMPREHENSION QUESTIONS ON PAGE 59:

1. (Possible response: Flowers produce fruits that contain seeds; seeds grow into new plants.) INFERENTIAL: SUMMARIZE
2. (Responses will vary.) CRITICAL: EXPRESS PERSONAL OPINIONS
3. (Possible response: Photographs can sometimes show real-life things more clearly than drawings.) CRITICAL: RECOGNIZE AUTHOR'S PURPOSE

Response to the Literature

WRITING Children's reports should include some interesting facts about the plant they chose. Reports should be written in complete sentences and paragraph format.

Name ______________________________

Flowers, Fruits, Seeds

Answer with complete sentences.

1. What are the main purposes of flowers, fruits, and seeds?

____

____

____

2. Learn the names of several plants in your home, yard, or neighborhood. Which is your favorite and why?

____

____

____

3. Why do you think the author of this book used photographs instead of drawings?

____

____

____

RESPONSE TO THE LITERATURE

WRITING Choose one plant from the book that you would like to know more about. Use an encyclopedia, the Internet, or other books to find out more about it. Write some interesting facts about your plant. Use complete sentences in a paragraph. Add some illustrations.

Reading Level

Summary

A young boy and his sister live through the morning their family leaves the neighborhood for a new home. They have already spent days saying good-bye to neighbors, friends, and relatives. Now all that remains is to watch the movers, share a moment in the empty apartment, and leave lip prints on the window before traveling on.

Author Information

Angela Johnson has collaborated with artist David Soman on several other family stories. Her book *Toning the Sweep* won her the Coretta Scott King Author Award, and *The Leaving Morning* was a Child Study Association Book of the Year.

More Books by Angela Johnson

The Aunt in Our House

The Girl Who Wore Snakes

Joshua by the Sea

Mama Bird, Baby Birds

Joshua's Night Whispers

The Leaving Morning

by Angela Johnson

Introducing the Book

You may wish to ask children the following questions to **build background** and **introduce story vocabulary.**

- What does it mean if you are leaving a place?
- Why do some people hire movers when they move?
- Have you ever packed a box or suitcase? What did you put in it?
- What is the difference between an apartment and a house?
- What is a street sweeper? How does this machine work?

SETTING A PURPOSE Display the book cover and some of the pictures. Tell children that one purpose for reading is to be entertained. Have them set a purpose for reading *The Leaving Morning*. If they have difficulty setting a purpose, offer this suggestion:

> MODEL **The pictures show a family packing boxes. I'll read to find out whether they are moving away and why.**

Reading Options

DIRECTED READING Use the Monitor Comprehension questions and Guided Reading strategies on pages 61–62 to check children's comprehension. WHOLE CLASS/SMALL GROUP

INDEPENDENT READING Have children read *The Leaving Morning* and complete the comprehension questions on page 63 independently. Encourage children to write their reactions to the story in their Reading Logs. INDIVIDUAL/WHOLE CLASS

Monitor Comprehension

Use these questions to monitor children's comprehension and evaluate their use of reading strategies.

Pages 1–5

1. **What do you think the author means by the "leaving morning"?** (Possible response: the time when someone is leaving) INFERENTIAL: DRAW CONCLUSIONS
2. **What kind of day is the leaving morning?** (Possible responses: soupy, misty, foggy, wet, quiet, cold, sad) INFERENTIAL: UNDERSTAND FIGURATIVE LANGUAGE
3. **What does the illustration on pages 4 and 5 tell you about the two children?** (Possible responses: They have been packing to move away; they look a little sad.) INFERENTIAL: USE PICTURE CLUES

Guided Reading

FOCUS STRATEGY **USE PRIOR KNOWLEDGE** If children have difficulty understanding the connection between the illustrations depicting a moving day and the characters' sad expressions, point out that they can use what they already know from firsthand or secondary experience about packing up and leaving for a new home to help them.

Monitor Comprehension

Pages 6–17

4. **Whom had the family said goodbye to?** (Possible responses: everyone they know; their friends, the grocer, everybody in their building, and the cousins) INFERENTIAL: SUMMARIZE
5. **Why do you think the author writes, "And the cousins, especially the cousins"?** (Possible response: It is very hard to say good-bye to the cousins because they will miss them a lot.) INFERENTIAL: DETERMINE AUTHOR'S PURPOSE
6. **Look back at the pictures. How do you think the children feel as they say good-bye to everyone?** (Possible response: With most people they look happy, but in a few pictures they look sad.) INFERENTIAL: USE PICTURE CLUES

Guided Reading

FOCUS STRATEGY **USE PICTURE CLUES TO CONFIRM MEANING** Ask children how the picture on pages 10 and 11 helped them make sure they read the word *grocer* correctly. (The picture shows a market. The children are talking to a man who works there.)

Monitor Comprehension

Pages 18–23

7. **Who is the family waiting for on the leaving morning?** (the movers) LITERAL: NOTE DETAILS

8. **What is the family doing at the deli?** (Possible response: having cocoa and watching for the movers) INFERENTIAL: DRAW CONCLUSIONS

Guided Reading

MAKE PREDICTIONS Give children the opportunity to predict what will happen in the next part of the story.

Monitor Comprehension

Pages 24–28

9. **How close did your predictions come to what happens?** (Responses will vary.) INFERENTIAL: CONFIRM PREDICTIONS

10. **How does the children's father make them feel better about moving?** (Possible response: He says that in a little while they will be someplace they will love.) INFERENTIAL: DRAW CONCLUSIONS

RETELLING Guidelines for performing a retelling of the story, as well as a rubric for evaluating the retelling, are provided on pages 110–111 of this teacher's guide.

ANSWERS TO COMPREHENSION QUESTIONS ON PAGE 63:

1. (Possible response: They are sad when they say good-bye, they know their things will be safe, and their parents are excited about the place they are moving to.) INFERENTIAL: SUMMARIZE
2. (Responses will vary.) CRITICAL: EXPRESS PERSONAL OPINIONS
3. (Possible response: She probably wrote it for children who are moving so that they would feel better about their move.) CRITICAL: RECOGNIZE AUTHOR'S PURPOSE

Response to the Literature

WRITING Children should include facts about the place they chose, and they should use complete sentences and paragraph format.

Name ____________________

The Leaving Morning

Answer with complete sentences.

1. How does the family feel on the leaving morning?

____

____

____

____

2. If you were moving, whom would you say good-bye to?

____

____

____

3. Whom do you think the author mainly wrote this book for, and why?

____

____

____

RESPONSE TO THE LITERATURE

WRITING If you could move anywhere in the world for a short time, where would you move? Find out about this place in books or an encyclopedia, or on the Internet. On another sheet of paper, write a paragraph describing the place. Tell why you would like to go there and what you would like to do there. Write your paragraph in complete sentences.

Reading Level

Summary

Whenever his grandfather visits, the narrator asks him to retell the tale of his trip to the moon. As Grandpa tells the story, the narrator imagines himself as being on the journey—blasting off, touching down on the lunar surface, taking the lunar rover out to gather rocks, planting a flag in the ground, and returning to Earth with a final splashdown.

Author Information

Timothy R. Gaffney is a reporter, pilot, and science writer who wrote this book as a means of preserving the stories of the moon voyagers who visited the lunar surface in the late 1960s and early 1970s.

More Books by Timothy R. Gaffney

Chuck Yeager: First Man to Fly Faster Than Sound

Edmund Hillary

Kennedy Space Center

Grandpa Takes Me to the Moon

by Timothy R. Gaffney

Introducing the Book

You may wish to ask children the following questions to **build background** and **introduce story vocabulary.**

- Would you like to travel into space? Why or why not?
- What do you already know about a rocket?
- Astronauts sit in a capsule at the top of a rocket. What do you think it is like in there?
- Why does a rocket need fuel?
- How does your weight on Earth compare to your weight in space?
- What is an orbit?
- What does a crater look like?

SETTING A PURPOSE Display the book cover and show children some of the pictures. Tell children that one purpose for reading is to be informed. Have them set a purpose for reading *Grandpa Takes Me to the Moon.* If they have difficulty setting a purpose, offer this suggestion:

> MODEL **The picture on the cover shows a boy and his grandfather in spacesuits on the moon. I'll read to find out about their trip.**

Reading Options

DIRECTED READING Use the Monitor Comprehension questions and the Guided Reading strategies on pages 65–66 to check children's comprehension. WHOLE CLASS/SMALL GROUP

INDEPENDENT READING Have children read *Grandpa Takes Me to the Moon* and complete the comprehension questions on page 67 independently. Encourage children to write their reactions to the story in their Reading Logs. INDIVIDUAL/WHOLE CLASS

Monitor Comprehension

Use these questions to monitor children's comprehension and evaluate their use of reading strategies.

Pages 3–9

1. **Why do you think the boy prefers to have his grandfather tell him about going to the moon?** (Possible response: The boy's grandfather may be able to make the story more exciting because it really happened to him.) CRITICAL: INTERPRET CHARACTERS' MOTIVATIONS
2. **Does the boy really go to the moon with his grandfather? Explain your answer.** (Possible response: No; the boy imagines himself going to the moon as his grandfather tells him a bedtime story.) CRITICAL: DISTINGUISH BETWEEN FANTASY AND REALITY
3. **What is the rocket like?** (Possible responses: very tall, has engines and fuel, has a tiny capsule at the top) LITERAL: NOTE DETAILS

Guided Reading

FOCUS STRATEGY **USE CONTEXT TO CONFIRM MEANING** Ask children what they should do if they aren't sure they read a word correctly. (They should look at the words around it.) Point out that this strategy will tell them whether the word they read makes sense.

Monitor Comprehension

Pages 10–15

4. **Why do the boy and his grandfather float in the capsule?** (Possible responses: There is no gravity in space; the boy doesn't feel his weight.) INFERENTIAL: CAUSE-EFFECT
5. **How do the boy and his grandfather land on the moon?** (Possible response: They float into a smaller spaceship called a moon lander. They fire the moon lander's rocket and drop slowly toward the moon until they land.) INFERENTIAL: SUMMARIZE
6. **Why is the sky they see from the moon as black as night?** (There is no air on the moon to make the sky blue.) LITERAL: NOTE DETAILS

Guided Reading

FOCUS STRATEGY **SELF-CORRECT** Ask children what they can do if they didn't read a word correctly. (They can correct themselves to make sure the letters in the word match the way they read it.)

Monitor Comprehension

Pages 16–23

7. **Name three ways the moon is different from the Earth.** (Possible responses: There are no green trees or grass, no brown rivers, no blue lakes, no white clouds, no wind, no air.) INFERENTIAL: COMPARE AND CONTRAST
8. **What is a lunar rover?** (Possible response: a buggy used to drive on around the moon) INFERENTIAL: IMPORTANT DETAILS
9. **Why do you think the boy and his grandfather take soil and rocks from the moon?** (Possible responses: to show others; to study on Earth) INFERENTIAL: SPECULATE

Guided Reading

MAKE PREDICTIONS Give children the opportunity to predict what will happen in the next part of the story.

Monitor Comprehension

Pages 24–30

10. **How close did your predictions come to what happens?** (Responses will vary.) INFERENTIAL: CONFIRM PREDICTIONS
11. **Why do you think they plant an American flag on the moon?** (Possible response: to prove Americans had been there) INFERENTIAL: SPECULATE
12. **Why do you think the author wrote this story?** (Possible response: He was excited about space travel and wanted to tell children about it.) CRITICAL: RECOGNIZE AUTHOR'S PURPOSE

RETELLING Guidelines for performing a retelling of the story, as well as a rubric for evaluating the retelling, are provided on pages 110–111 of this teacher's guide.

ANSWERS TO COMPREHENSION QUESTIONS ON PAGE 67:

1. (Possible response: He and his grandfather get into the capsule, blast off, land on the moon, walk on the moon, plant a flag on the moon, return to Earth with soil and rocks from the moon.) INFERENTIAL: SUMMARIZE
2. (Responses will vary.) CRITICAL: EXPRESS PERSONAL OPINIONS
3. (Possible response: because it gives the reader an idea of what it would be like to really go there) CRITICAL: LITERARY ANALYSIS

Response to the Literature

WRITING Before they begin their reviews, tell children to write down three words that they will want to use to describe the book. Children should use complete sentences and paragraph format in their book reviews.

Name ________________________________

Grandpa Takes Me to the Moon

Answer with complete sentences.

1. What important events happen on the boy's trip to the moon?

____

____

____

____

2. Would you like to go on a trip to space? Why or why not?

____

____

____

3. Why do you think the author mixed real facts about the moon with an imaginary story about going there?

____

____

____

RESPONSE TO THE LITERATURE

WRITING Write a book review about *Grandpa Takes Me to the Moon.* Make your book review so exciting someone will want to read the book. In your book review, tell a little about the book and why you liked it. Use complete sentences in a paragraph.

Reading Level

Summary

Whether there's an emergency at sea, on a snowy mountain, or in a burning house, rescue experts help save lives and property. Firefighters, police officers, paramedics, and others in these important jobs race to the scene in their well-equipped vehicles. Have a look at motorcycles, police cars, ambulances, fire trucks, boats, and helicopters in this informative book.

Author/Illustrator Information

Gail Gibbons is the author and illustrator of *Emergency!* and more than 50 other nonfiction children's books on a wide range of topics. "The book has to be about something the kids find intriguing," says Gibbons. "It also has to be about something that makes me curious."

More Books by Gail Gibbons

Nature's Green Umbrella

The Honey Maker

Bicycle Book

Exploring the Deep, Dark Sea

The Art Box

Wolves

Emergency!

by Gail Gibbons

Introducing the Book

You may wish to ask children the following questions to **build background** and to **introduce story vocabulary.**

- What is an emergency?
- What are ambulances used for? What do sirens sound like?
- If there is a crime or an accident, who helps?
- What do paramedics do?
- Where can you find a fire hydrant?
- How is your arm similar to a boom on a fire truck?

SETTING A PURPOSE Display the book cover, and show children some of the pictures. Tell children that one purpose for reading is to be informed. Have them set a purpose for reading *Emergency!* If they have difficulty setting a purpose, offer this suggestion:

> MODEL **The pictures show many kinds of vehicles: motorcycles, ambulances, police cars, fire trucks, boats, and aircraft. I'll read to find out how these vehicles and the people in them help out in emergencies.**

Reading Options

DIRECTED READING Use the Monitor Comprehension questions and Guided Reading strategies on pages 69–70 to check children's comprehension. WHOLE CLASS/SMALL GROUP

INDEPENDENT READING Have children read *Emergency!* and complete the comprehension questions on page 71 independently. Encourage children to write their reactions to the story in their Reading Logs. INDIVIDUAL/WHOLE CLASS

Monitor Comprehension

Use these questions to monitor children's comprehension and evaluate their use of reading strategies.

Pages 1–7

1. **What are the four emergencies shown on page 1?** (Possible response: a robbery, a fire, people stranded in a boat, and people lost in a snowstorm) INFERENTIAL: USE PICTURE CLUES
2. **Why do police cars use sirens and flashing lights?** (Possible response: to warn other drivers to get out of the way because they are in a hurry) INFERENTIAL: CAUSE-EFFECT
3. **Which vehicle would help more after a car accident, a rescue unit vehicle or a police motorcycle? Why?** (Possible response: a rescue unit vehicle; because it has special equipment that can be used to help injured people) INFERENTIAL: COMPARE AND CONTRAST

Guided Reading

FOCUS STRATEGY **REREAD** Ask children what they should do if they are confused about something they read in the story. (They should reread that part of the story.) Point out to children that by rereading, they may notice important details they missed the first time that will help them understand the story.

Monitor Comprehension

Pages 8–11

4. **What are ambulances used for?** (Possible responses: They carry medical equipment and paramedics to care for sick or injured people; they take people to hospitals quickly.) INFERENTIAL: SUMMARIZE
5. **Look at the pictures on pages 10 and 11. How does a boom work?** (Possible response: It opens up to lift the worker up high.) INFERENTIAL: IMPORTANT DETAILS
6. **Did the author write about facts or her own opinion? How do you know?** (Possible response: facts; because she wrote about things that really happen) METACOGNITIVE: DISTINGUISH FACT FROM OPINION

Guided Reading

FOCUS STRATEGY **USE PICTURE CLUES TO CONFIRM MEANING** Ask children how they can use the pictures to help them make sure they read the words correctly. (The pictures show what the words mean.) Point out that if they are confused by the words, the pictures give clues to the meaning of the words.

Monitor Comprehension

Pages 12–17

7. **Why is a tanker truck first to arrive at a fire?** (Possible response: because it carries its own water and can start putting out the fire right away) INFERENTIAL: DRAW CONCLUSIONS

8. **How does a pumper truck work?** (Possible response: It pumps water from a fire hydrant or other water source. The water goes through hoses into the truck. Pumps in the truck push the water through discharge hoses onto the fire.) INFERENTIAL: SUMMARIZE

9. **What are the four kinds of fire trucks?** (tanker trucks, pumper trucks, aerial ladder trucks, and platform trucks) LITERAL: NOTE DETAILS

Guided Reading

FOCUS STRATEGY **SELF-CORRECT** Tell children that sometimes when a word doesn't make sense, they might notice that the letters in the word do not match the way they have read it. Have children correct themselves when this happens by looking carefully at the word and rereading it.

Monitor Comprehension

Pages 18–27

10. **Why might a Coast Guard helicopter be used to rescue someone instead of a Coast Guard boat?** (Possible response: because the water might be too rough for a boat, and a helicopter can arrive sooner) INFERENTIAL: MAKE COMPARISONS

11. **Why are emergency workers able to respond faster than ever before?** (Possible response: They have better communication, and their vehicles are faster.) INFERENTIAL: CAUSE-EFFECT

12. **Why do you think the author wrote this book?** (Possible response: to give information about the emergency vehicles and rescue workers we may have seen) INFERENTIAL: DETERMINE AUTHOR'S PURPOSE

RETELLING Guidelines for performing a retelling of the story, as well as a rubric for evaluating the retelling, are provided on pages 110–111 of this teacher's guide.

ANSWERS TO COMPREHENSION QUESTIONS ON PAGE 71:

1. (Possible response: because there are many kinds of emergencies that are in different places and need special types of equipment) INFERENTIAL: SUMMARIZE
2. (Responses will vary.) CRITICAL: EXPRESS PERSONAL OPINIONS
3. (Possible response: She may have read about them, talked to rescue crews, and watched them work.) CRITICAL: INTERPRET AUTHOR'S VIEWPOINT

Response to the Literature

WRITING Children's posters should show several types of emergency vehicles labeled. Children should use complete sentences to tell about each vehicle.

Name ______________________

Emergency!

Answer with complete sentences.

1. Why is it important to have many kinds of emergency rescue vehicles?

____

____

____

2. If you could spend a day working with one of the rescue workers you read about, which one would it be? Explain your answer.

____

____

____

3. What do you think Gail Gibbons did to get information about the emergency vehicles and the people who work in them?

____

____

____

RESPONSE TO THE LITERATURE

WRITING There are many kinds of emergency vehicles. Each one is important in helping people. Make a list of the vehicles in *Emergency!* Then, make a poster that shows as many of the vehicles as you wish. Draw the vehicles and label them. Write one or two sentences about each one. Give your poster a title.

Reading Level

Summary

Attacked by an owl while flying with her mother, fruit bat Stellaluna falls into a bird's nest and is raised as a nestling by the mother bird. At first, the bat balks at eating insects, resting upright, and sleeping at night, but she adapts to the birds' schedule and finds herself well cared for. When the birds and Stellaluna learn to fly, she is reunited with her mother and the other bats. She finds that the differences between bats and birds do not matter as much as their similarities and friendship.

Author/Illustrator Information

In addition to *Stellaluna*, **Janell Cannon** is the author-illustrator of *Trupp: A Fuzzhead Tale*, which describes the adventures of the gentle, intelligent Fuzzheads as they explore the human world. Ms. Cannon lives in southern California.

Stellaluna

by Janell Cannon

Introducing the Book

You may wish to ask children the following questions to **build background** and to **introduce story vocabulary.**

- What kind of animal is a bat?
- What is a wing used for?
- What kind of animal lives in a nest?
- How are bats different from birds?
- How are bats and birds alike?
- Why do you think a bat flies in the nighttime instead of during the day?
- When is an owl awake?
- What does it mean to rescue someone?

SETTING A PURPOSE Display the book cover, read the title, and point out that *Stellaluna* is the name of the bat on the cover. Then show children some of the story illustrations. Tell children that one purpose for reading is to be entertained. Have them set a purpose for reading *Stellaluna*. If children have difficulty setting a purpose, offer this suggestion:

> MODEL **The pictures show birds and bats. I know one bat is Stellaluna. I'll read to find out what happens to this bat.**

Reading Options

DIRECTED READING Use the Monitor Comprehension questions and the Guided Reading strategies on pages 73–74 to check children's comprehension. WHOLE CLASS/SMALL GROUP

INDEPENDENT READING Have children read *Stellaluna* and complete the comprehension questions on page 75 independently. Encourage children to write their reactions to the story in their Reading Logs. INDIVIDUAL/WHOLE CLASS

Monitor Comprehension

Use these questions to monitor children's comprehension and to evaluate their use of reading strategies.

Pages 3–11

1. **How does Stellaluna get separated from her mother?** (Possible response: An owl swoops down on them, and Stellaluna falls out of her mother's grasp.) INFERENTIAL: SUMMARIZE
2. **Why does Stellaluna fall instead of fly?** (Possible response: Her baby wings are limp and useless; she doesn't know how to fly yet.) INFERENTIAL: IMPORTANT DETAILS
3. **Why doesn't Stellaluna want to eat the crawly things the birds eat?** (Possible response: She is a fruit bat; she eats only ripe fruit, not bugs.) INFERENTIAL: DRAW CONCLUSIONS

Guided Reading

FOCUS STRATEGY **LOOK AT WORD BITS AND PARTS** Tell children that one way to figure out an unfamiliar word is to look for smaller words they know inside the longer word. Children may apply this strategy to reading words such as *daybreak*, *headfirst*, and *grasshopper*.

Monitor Comprehension

Pages 12–23

4. **How does Stellaluna learn to be like the birds?** (She stays awake all day, sleeps at night, and eats bugs.) LITERAL: NOTE DETAILS
5. **What does Stellaluna teach the birds to do?** (Possible response: hang by their feet outside the nest) INFERENTIAL: IMPORTANT DETAILS
6. **Why do you think Stellaluna has trouble flying?** (Responses will vary.) CRITICAL: SPECULATE

Guided Reading

FOCUS STRATEGY **LOOK FOR WORDS YOU KNOW** Ask children what they should do if they find words they don't know. (They should find words they do know to help them figure out the unfamiliar ones.)

Monitor Comprehension

Pages 24–31

7. **Why doesn't Stellaluna know that she is a bat?** (Possible response: She thinks she is a bird because she has been living with birds.) INFERENTIAL: DETERMINE CHARACTERS' EMOTIONS

8. **Why does the mother bat sniff Stellaluna's fur?** (Possible response: Sniffing helps her find out if this really is her baby. Mother animals use their sense of smell to find their babies.) CRITICAL: CLASSIFY

9. **How do you think Stellaluna will feel about the birds now that she has found her mother and the other bats?** (Responses will vary.) INFERENTIAL: MAKE PREDICTIONS

Guided Reading

MAKE PREDICTIONS Give children the opportunity to predict what will happen in the next part of the story.

Monitor Comprehension

Pages 32–45

10. **How close did your predictions come to what happens?** (Responses will vary.) INFERENTIAL: CONFIRM PREDICTIONS

11. **In what ways are bats and birds different?** (Possible responses: Bats fly at night; birds fly by day. Bats can see at night, but birds can't. Bats hang upside down to sleep; baby birds sleep in a nest.) INFERENTIAL: COMPARE AND CONTRAST

12. **Why do you think the author included "Bat Notes" in the book?** (Possible response: to give some facts about bats) CRITICAL: INTERPRET TEXT STRUCTURE

RETELLING Guidelines for performing a retelling of the story, as well as a rubric for evaluating the retelling, are provided on pages 110–111 of this teacher's guide.

ANSWERS TO COMPREHENSION QUESTIONS ON PAGE 75:

1. (Possible responses: They learn how different they are and how alike they are. They also learn that they can be friends even though they are different.) INFERENTIAL: SUMMARIZE

2. (Responses will vary.) CRITICAL: EXPRESS PERSONAL OPINIONS

3. (Possible response: to hibernate, to eat honey) INFERENTIAL: SYNTHESIZE

Response to the Literature

WRITING Children should use complete sentences in their paragraph and include interesting facts about bats.

Name ______________________________

Stellaluna

Answer with complete sentences.

1. What do you think Stellaluna and the baby birds learn from each other by the end of the story?

___

___

___

2. What do you think it means when the birds say, "How can we be so different and feel so much alike?"

___

___

___

3. Stellaluna's stay with the bird family teaches her a lot about how birds live. What might she learn if she visited a bear family next?

___

___

___

RESPONSE TO THE LITERATURE

WRITING Think about what you learned about bats as you read *Stellaluna*. On another sheet of paper, write some interesting facts you learned about bats. Write complete sentences in a paragraph.

Reading Level

Summary

Although his brother Sol laughs at him, young Ernst the crocodile refuses to collect starfish or bottle caps, choosing to collect puddles instead. As he merges the colorful puddles in his bucket, Ernst finds that his collection is useful for making watercolor pictures and quenching the thirst of a wandering dog.

Author/Illustrator Information

Elisa Kleven is the illustrator of the award-winning *Abuela* as well as its sequel, *Isla*. She is also the author-illustrator of *The Paper Princess*. Kleven lives in Albany, California.

More Books by Elisa Kleven

Ernst

Hooray, a Piñata!

The Lion and the Little Red Bird

The Puddle Pail

by Elisa Kleven

Introducing the Book

You may wish to ask children the following questions to **build background** and to **introduce story vocabulary.**

- What are some interesting things to collect?
- What kind of collection would you like to have?
- How is an apple different from a grape?
- What can you use a pail for?

SETTING A PURPOSE Display the book cover, and ask children what a puddle pail might be. Then show them some of the story illustrations. Tell children that one purpose for reading is to be entertained. Have them set a purpose for reading *The Puddle Pail*. If children have difficulty setting a purpose, offer this suggestion:

> MODEL **The pictures show two crocodiles putting things in their pails. I'll read to find out what these characters decide to collect.**

Reading Options

DIRECTED READING Use the Monitor Comprehension questions and Guided Reading strategies on pages 77–78 to check children's comprehension. WHOLE CLASS/SMALL GROUP

INDEPENDENT READING Have children read *The Puddle Pail* and complete the comprehension questions on page 79 independently. Encourage children to write their reactions to the story in their Reading Logs. INDIVIDUAL/WHOLE CLASS

Monitor Comprehension

Use these questions to monitor children's comprehension and evaluate their use of reading strategies.

Pages 2–9

1. **What does Sol love to do and what does Ernst love to do?** (Sol loves to collect things. Ernst loves to make things.) LITERAL: MAKE COMPARISONS
2. **What are some of the collections Sol has?** (Possible responses: shells, rocks, feathers, string, rubber bands) INFERENTIAL: CLASSIFY
3. **Do you think collecting cookies is a good idea for Ernst? Why or why not?** (Possible response: No, because he would probably eat them.) INFERENTIAL: SPECULATE

Guided Reading

FOCUS STRATEGY **REREAD** Ask children what they should do if they are confused about something they read in the story. (They should reread that part of the story.) Point out that by rereading, children may notice important details they missed the first time that will help them understand the story.

Monitor Comprehension

Pages 10–17

4. **Where does Ernst get the idea to collect puddles?** (He looks at a bottle cap that is lying in a puddle.) LITERAL: NOTE DETAILS
5. **What do you think of a puddle collection?** (Responses will vary.) CRITICAL: EXPRESS PERSONAL OPINIONS
6. **Why does each puddle that Ernst collects look different?** (because each one is reflecting something different) INFERENTIAL: CAUSE-EFFECT

Guided Reading

FOCUS STRATEGY **USE PICTURE CLUES TO CONFIRM MEANING** Ask children what they should do if they are not sure they read the adjectives describing each puddle correctly. (They should use the pictures to make sure.)

Monitor Comprehension

Pages 18–23

7. **What do all the colorful puddles look like in Ernst's pail?** (They are just a pail full of water.) LITERAL: NOTE DETAILS
8. **Why does Ernst's puddle change colors?** (Possible response: It reflects the sky.) INFERENTIAL: CAUSE-EFFECT

Guided Reading

MAKE PREDICTIONS Give children the opportunity to predict what will happen in the next part of the story.

Monitor Comprehension

Pages 24–30

9. **How close did your predictions come to what happens?** (Responses will vary.) INFERENTIAL: CONFIRM PREDICTIONS
10. **How does Ernst use his puddle collection?** (to paint watercolor pictures) LITERAL: NOTE DETAILS
11. **By the end of the story, how does Sol feel about Ernst's collection? How do you know?** (Possible response: He likes it; because he says, "Oooh! What a collection!") INFERENTIAL: DETERMINE CHARACTERS' EMOTIONS

RETELLING Guidelines for performing a retelling of the story, as well as a rubric for evaluating the retelling, are provided on pages 110–111 of this teacher's guide.

ANSWERS TO COMPREHENSION QUESTIONS ON PAGE 79:

1. (Possible response: Sol still wants to collect things he can sort into boxes, and Ernst tries to collect a shadow, which he can't carry home.) INFERENTIAL: SUMMARIZE
2. (Responses will vary.) CRITICAL: EXPRESS PERSONAL OPINIONS
3. (Possible responses: to show we are all different and like different things; that we should appreciate differences in one another) CRITICAL: RECOGNIZE AUTHOR'S PURPOSE

Response to the Literature

WRITING Before children begin, have them brainstorm a list of unusual things to collect. Children should use complete sentences and paragraph format.

Name ______________________________

The Puddle Pail

Answer with complete sentences.

1. At the end of the story, how do you know each character still loves the things he did at the beginning of the story?

____

____

____

2. Would you rather go out collecting with Sol or Ernst? Why?

____

____

____

3. Why do you think the author made the collections of each crocodile so different?

____

____

____

RESPONSE TO THE LITERATURE

WRITING Ernst collected interesting things in his pail. On another sheet of paper, write a story about what you would like to collect in a pail. Think of something that is interesting and unusual. Use complete sentences in a paragraph.

Reading Level

Summary

Fernando plans to spend his vacation painting. He mixes paints the way his teacher told him to, but he has no paper to paint on. When he asks to paint on the family's adobe house, his parents are hesitant, but they finally agree. His neighbors are so impressed by his fanciful, colorful work that they all ask him to decorate their houses as well.

Author Information

Patricia Maloney Markun heard the story of the young painter of Sabana Grande when she was living in Panama. She visited his village and saw his art, and that inspired her to write his story. She is also the author of several nonfiction books for children and now lives in Washington, D.C.

More Books by Patricia Maloney Markun

Central America and Panama (First Book)

Panama Canal: A First Book

Mystery on Taboga Island

The Little Painter of Sabana Grande

by Patricia Maloney Markun

Introducing the Book

You may wish to ask children the following questions to **build background** and **introduce story vocabulary.**

- What is adobe used for?
- What do you think an artist might use charcoal for?
- What is something you can make from clay?
- What is a toucan? Where could you see one?
- What is a sloth? How does it move?
- What kinds of plants have blossoms?
- What do you think a thatched roof is made of?

SETTING A PURPOSE Display the book cover and point out the main character, Fernando. Remind children that they can read to learn about other people and places. Have children set a purpose for reading. If they have difficulty setting a purpose, offer this suggestion:

> MODEL **I wonder whether Fernando is the painter in the story. I'll read to find out how he becomes a painter and what he paints.**

Reading Options

DIRECTED READING Use the Monitor Comprehension questions and Guided Reading strategies on pages 81–82 to check children's comprehension. WHOLE CLASS/SMALL GROUP

INDEPENDENT READING Have children read *The Little Painter of Sabana Grande* and complete the comprehension questions on page 83 independently. Encourage children to write their reactions to the story in their Reading Logs. INDIVIDUAL/WHOLE CLASS

Monitor Comprehension

Use these questions to monitor children's comprehension and evaluate their use of reading strategies.

Pages 2–9

1. **What is Sabana Grande?** (It is a small village in Panama, just seven adobe houses beside a brook in a meadow.) LITERAL: NOTE DETAILS
2. **Where does Fernando get his paints?** (Possible response: from nature: black from the charcoal of a burned tree stump, blue from berries, yellow from dried grass, red from brook clay) INFERENTIAL: SUMMARIZE
3. **What problem does Fernando have to solve?** (Possible response: There is no paper in his village to draw on.) INFERENTIAL: IMPORTANT DETAILS

Guided Reading

FOCUS STRATEGY **REREAD** Ask children what they can do if they forget a detail or realize they don't understand what they've read. (They can go back and reread to find information.) Explain that rereading is an important strategy for understanding both fiction and nonfiction.

Monitor Comprehension

Pages 10–15

4. **What does Fernando do about the paper problem?** (Possible response: He decides to paint on the smooth, white adobe walls of his house.) INFERENTIAL: IMPORTANT DETAILS
5. **What do Fernando's parents say about his plan at first?** (They say no.) LITERAL: NOTE DETAILS
6. **Why do Fernando's parents change their minds?** (Possible response: His father can't stand to see Fernando so miserable. His mother wants him to do his best.) INFERENTIAL: DETERMINE CHARACTERS' MOTIVATIONS

Guided Reading

FOCUS STRATEGY **MAKE INFERENCES** Have children review what has happened in the story so far and tell how they think Fernando feels about each of these events: learning there is no paper, having a great idea, hearing his parents say no, hearing them say yes. Ask how readers can tell what Fernando is feeling. (words, pictures, personal experience) Explain that when readers put what they read together with what they already know, they can better understand something an author does not say.

Monitor Comprehension

Pages 16–21

7. **What does Fernando do before he starts painting the big picture?** (He paints a tiny plan of what he will paint.) LITERAL: SEQUENCE

8. **What is in the picture Fernando paints?** (Possible response: plants and animals he knows—poinciana tree, toucan, sloth—and a vine) INFERENTIAL: IMPORTANT DETAILS

9. **What do the neighbors do while Fernando is painting?** (Possible response: They ask questions, watch, and spread the word about the little painter.) INFERENTIAL: SUMMARIZE

Guided Reading

MAKE PREDICTIONS Give children the opportunity to predict what will happen in the next part of the story.

Monitor Comprehension

Pages 22–30

10. **How did your predictions compare to what happens?** (Responses will vary.) INFERENTIAL: CONFIRM PREDICTIONS

11. **How do people show that they like Fernando's painting?** (Possible responses: His teacher says he did very well; his neighbors say kind things and ask him to paint their houses.) INFERENTIAL: DETERMINE CHARACTERS' EMOTIONS

12. **How does Fernando feel at the end of the story?** (Possible responses: proud of his work, happy that he can go on painting) INFERENTIAL: DETERMINE CHARACTERS' EMOTIONS

RETELLING Guidelines for performing a retelling of the story, as well as a rubric for evaluating the retelling, are provided on pages 110–111 of this teacher's guide.

ANSWERS TO COMPREHENSION QUESTIONS ON PAGE 83:

1. (Possible response: Fernando learns to paint at school. His teacher gives him brushes and tells him how to make paint. When he can't find paper, he paints on the walls of his house.) INFERENTIAL: SUMMARIZE
2. (Responses will vary.) CRITICAL: EXPRESS PERSONAL OPINIONS
3. (Possible response: Don't give up on your dreams even when they seem impossible.) CRITICAL: INTERPRET THEME

Response to the Literature

WRITING Children's paragraphs should tell about a special talent they have: how they recognized it, why they enjoy it, and how they use it. Children should write in complete sentences.

Name ______________________________

The Little Painter of Sabana Grande

Answer with complete sentences.

1. How does Fernando become a painter?

____

____

____

2. If you could paint on a building, what would you paint a picture of?

____

____

____

3. What do you think the author wanted readers to learn from this story?

____

____

____

RESPONSE TO THE LITERATURE

WRITING Write a paragraph that describes something you do well. Explain how you learned to do it. Tell why you like it. Use complete sentences in your final draft.

Julian, Dream Doctor

by Ann Cameron

Reading Level

Summary

Julian wants to give his dad the birthday present of his dreams. After a series of amusing attempts, Julian *thinks* he learns what his dad wants most: two snakes. Julian succeeds in catching the snakes and keeping them for the big day. While they live in his room, he learns not to be afraid of them. When his dad opens the gift, he yells and runs out of the house. With Julian's example and encouragement from the family, Julian's dad overcomes his lifelong fear of snakes, and the gift turns out to be a good one after all.

Author Information

Ann Cameron was born in the United States and lives in Guatemala. She has always had an interest in other cultures and in the "things we have in common as human beings." She sees her character Julian as "a child whose hopes and mishaps children everywhere can understand." Readers' letters tell her they agree. Cameron is the volunteer supervisor of her local library.

More Books by Ann Cameron

The Stories Julian Tells

More Stories Julian Tells

Julian's Glorious Summer

Julian, Secret Agent

Introducing the Book

You may wish to ask children the following questions to **build background** and **introduce story vocabulary.**

- What does it mean to say someone dreams of having a pet?
- What does it mean to imagine something?
- How do you keep a secret?
- What makes something a surprise?
- What decorations might you see at a birthday party?
- What is a birthday present for a friend?

SETTING A PURPOSE Display the book cover, read the title, and point out Julian. Remind children that one purpose for reading is to be entertained. Have them set a purpose for reading. If they have difficulty setting a purpose, offer this suggestion:

MODEL **The title of the book says that Julian is a dream doctor. I'll read to find out what that means.**

Reading Options

DIRECTED READING Use the Monitor comprehension questions and the Guided Reading strategies on pages 85–86 to check children's comprehension. WHOLE CLASS/SMALL GROUP

INDEPENDENT READING Have children read *Julian, Dream Doctor* and complete the comprehension questions on page 87 independently. Encourage children to write their reactions to the story in their Reading Logs. INDIVIDUAL/WHOLE CLASS

Monitor Comprehension

Use these questions to monitor children's comprehension and evaluate their use of reading strategies.

Pages 5–15

1. **How does Julian describe his father and his mother?** (Possible response: His father is quick-moving, likes to play jokes, is full of surprises, is a good athlete, gets impatient; his mom never gets impatient, is a good listener, is never in a hurry, talks softly.) INFERENTIAL: COMPARE AND CONTRAST
2. **What is Julian's very good idea?** (Possible response: to get his father a special birthday present) INFERENTIAL: MAIN IDEA
3. **Why is Julian having a hard time deciding what to give his dad?** (Possible response: His dad loves things that are too big or too small to be gifts.) INFERENTIAL: DRAW CONCLUSIONS

Guided Reading

FOCUS STRATEGY **READ AHEAD** Ask children how they could figure out what an *atom* (page 13) is. (by reading ahead to find clues) Explain that reading ahead often gives clues to help readers better understand what they are reading.

Monitor Comprehension

Pages 16–33

4. **What does Julian do to try to read his dad's mind?** (Possible response: First, he makes a brain wave machine out of pots and pans and clothesline; next, he ties himself to his bed and goes out on the porch roof to use the TV antenna as a receiver.) INFERENTIAL: SEQUENCE
5. **How does Julian find out what his dad wants?** (Possible response: He makes his dad talk in his sleep.) INFERENTIAL: PROBLEM SOLVE
6. **What does Julian's father say he wants for his birthday?** ("Two snakes. Big ones.") LITERAL: NOTE DETAILS

Guided Reading

FOCUS STRATEGY **USE PRIOR KNOWLEDGE** If children have difficulty understanding why Julian is asking his sleeping father questions, point out that they can use what they already know about dreaming and talking in one's sleep to help them.

Monitor Comprehension

Pages 34–47

7. **How does Gloria help Julian and Huey on the snake hunt?** (Possible response: She reads them information about snakes, calms them down when they are scared, and catches one snake.) INFERENTIAL: SUMMARIZE

8. **How does Julian feel as he carries the snakes home?** (Amazed, amazed, amazed; he can hardly believe they succeeded.) LITERAL: IDENTIFY CHARACTERS' EMOTIONS

9. **How do Julian's feelings about the snakes change?** (Possible response: He gets less afraid because he keeps them in his room, takes care of them, and even touches them, and he realizes they won't hurt him.) INFERENTIAL: MAIN IDEA

Guided Reading

MAKE PREDICTIONS Give children the opportunity to predict what will happen in the next part of the story.

Monitor Comprehension

Pages 48–62

10. **How did your predictions compare to what happens?** (Answers will vary.) INFERENTIAL: CONFIRM PREDICTIONS

11. **What do Julian's dad and mom do when his dad gets the snakes?** (Possible response: His dad yells and runs out of the house because he is afraid of snakes; his mother stays calm, thinks about how the snakes might feel, and encourages Julian's dad to try to get used to them.) INFERENTIAL: COMPARE AND CONTRAST

12. **Why does Julian's dad call Julian a "dream doctor"?** (Possible response: Julian's present helps his dad get used to snakes so he can stop being afraid of them.) INFERENTIAL: CAUSE-EFFECT

RETELLING Guidelines for performing a retelling of the story, as well as a rubric for evaluating the retelling, are provided on pages 110–111 of this teacher's guide.

ANSWERS TO COMPREHENSION QUESTIONS ON PAGE 87:

1. (Possible answer: He catches two snakes and gives them to his dad. His dad is afraid of snakes, but he gets over his fear because Julian has gotten over his fear.) INFERENTIAL: SUMMARIZE

2. (Responses will vary.) CRITICAL: EXPRESS PERSONAL OPINIONS

3. (Possible response: Julian is loving because he wants to get his dad a special birthday present. He is brave because he catches the snakes even though he is afraid of them.) CRITICAL: INTERPRET CHARACTERS' MOTIVATIONS

Response to the Literature

WRITING Children's stories should tell about a surprise birthday present. Stories can be fiction or nonfiction. Each story should include at least one descriptive comparison. Children should write in complete sentences.

Name ______________________________

Julian, Dream Doctor

Answer with complete sentences.

1. How does Julian get his dad a birthday present? Why is it a special present?

____

____

____

____

2. What did you like best about this book?

____

____

____

____

3. What sort of person is Julian? How do you know?

____

____

____

____

RESPONSE TO THE LITERATURE

WRITING Write your own story about a surprise birthday present you gave or received. The story can be true or made up. Compare two people or things in your story. Use complete sentences.

Reading Level

Summary

Every year on his birthday, Pablo visits his grandfather, Lito *(Abuelito)*. Lito decorates a special tree he planted the year Pablo was adopted into the family. Pablo hears again the story of his arrival, and he and Lito remember how the tree has been decorated each year of his life.

Author Information

Pat Mora says, "Am I lucky! Because I grew up in a bilingual home, I speak two languages and can write in English and Spanish." She writes stories for children and poetry for children and adults. Her work has won many awards, particularly for giving voice to Hispanic American culture. She says, "I've always enjoyed reading all kinds of books, and now I get to write them too, to sit and play with words on my computer."

More Books by Pat Mora

A Birthday Basket for Tía

Confetti: Poems for Children

The Desert Is My Mother

The Race of the Toad and Deer

The Big Sky

Tomás and the Library Lady

Pablo's Tree

by Pat Mora

Introducing the Book

You may wish to ask children the following questions to **build background** and **introduce story vocabulary.**

- What does it mean to visit someone?
- What does it mean to say someone remembered your birthday?
- What does it mean to adopt a child?
- What is a tree nursery? What would you see there?
- What does it mean to welcome someone into a family?
- When is your birthday? How do you celebrate your birthday?

SETTING A PURPOSE Display the book cover and point out Pablo. Remind children that one purpose for reading is to be entertained. Have children set a purpose for reading. If they have difficulty setting a purpose, offer this suggestion:

> MODEL **The picture shows a boy, Pablo, and a little tree. I'll read to find out if the tree is special.**

Reading Options

DIRECTED READING Use the Monitor Comprehension questions and Guided Reading strategies on pages 89–90 to check children's comprehension. WHOLE CLASS/SMALL GROUP

INDEPENDENT READING Have children read *Pablo's Tree* and complete the comprehension questions on page 91 independently. Encourage children to write their reactions to the story in their Reading Logs. INDIVIDUAL/WHOLE CLASS

Monitor Comprehension

Use these questions to monitor children's comprehension and evaluate their use of reading strategies.

Pages 2–9

1. **Who is Lito?** (Pablo's grandfather/abuelito) LITERAL: NOTE DETAILS
2. **Why is Pablo going to his grandfather's house?** (Possible response: Pablo always spends the night after his birthday with his grandfather.) INFERENTIAL: CAUSE-EFFECT
3. **What does Lito do every year for Pablo's birthday?** (Possible response: He decorates Pablo's tree.) INFERENTIAL: IMPORTANT DETAILS

Guided Reading

FOCUS STRATEGY **READ AHEAD** Have children find the words written in Spanish on pages 8 and 9. Point out that children can read ahead to find the English translations of these unfamiliar words.

Monitor Comprehension

Pages 10–15

4. **What has Lito used to decorate the tree?** (Possible response: tiny colored bells and wind chimes) INFERENTIAL: IMPORTANT DETAILS
5. **What does Pablo's mother do after she sees the tree?** (Possible response: She kisses Pablo and Lito good-bye and leaves.) INFERENTIAL: SEQUENCE
6. **What is the story Lito tells Pablo?** (Possible response: Lito tells about buying the tree and waiting for the day Pablo would be adopted.) INFERENTIAL: SUMMARIZE

Guided Reading

FOCUS STRATEGY **SEQUENCE EVENTS/SUMMARIZE** Tell children to think about the order of story events as they read. Encourage them to think about what has already happened in the story. Then they can read on to find out what happens next.

Monitor Comprehension

Pages 16–23

7. **Where did Lito put the tree first?** (Possible response: by the front door to welcome Pablo) INFERENTIAL: SEQUENCE

8. **Why did Lito plant the tree?** (Possible response: to celebrate Pablo's arrival) INFERENTIAL: MAIN IDEA

Guided Reading

MAKE PREDICTIONS Give children the opportunity to predict what will happen in the next part of the story.

Monitor Comprehension

Pages 24–30

9. **How did Lito decorate the tree for each of Pablo's birthdays?** (1. streamers; 2. balloons; 3. paper lanterns; 4. birdcages; tiny colored bells and wind chimes) LITERAL: SEQUENCE

10. **Why won't Lito say what will be on the tree next year?** (Possible response: He wants it to be a surprise.) INFERENTIAL: CAUSE-EFFECT

11. **How do you know Pablo and his grandfather love each other?** (Possible response: They smile, hug, enjoy spending time together, and share the joy of Pablo's tree.) INFERENTIAL: DETERMINE CHARACTERS' EMOTIONS

RETELLING Guidelines for performing a retelling of the story, as well as a rubric for evaluating the retelling, are provided on pages 110–111 of this teacher's guide.

ANSWERS TO COMPREHENSION QUESTIONS ON PAGE 91:

1. (Possible response: The tree is special because Lito planted it on the day Pablo was adopted, and he decorates it every year for Pablo's birthday.) INFERENTIAL: SUMMARIZE

2. (Responses will vary.) CRITICAL: EXPRESS PERSONAL OPINIONS

3. (Possible response: The family includes Pablo, his mother, and his grandfather. They speak Spanish and English. They love each other.) INFERENTIAL: DETERMINE CHARACTERS' TRAITS

Response to the Literature

WRITING Before children begin, ask them to think about special people in their lives. These may include family members or close friends. Children's paragraphs should tell how they would decorate their trees, who they would be for, and how they would look when they were finished. Children should write in complete sentences.

Name ______________________________

Pablo's Tree

Answer the questions in complete sentences.

1. Why is Pablo's tree special?

____

____

____

____

2. If you could have a birthday tree decorated for your next birthday, what would you like to have on it?

____

____

____

3. How does the author describe Pablo's family?

____

____

____

____

RESPONSE TO THE LITERATURE

WRITING Suppose that you want to decorate a tree for someone you love. Write a paragraph that describes what you would do. Tell who the tree would be for. How would it look when you finished? Use complete sentences in your final copy.

Reading Level

Summary

Every day, the narrator and her mother walk along the beach near their home. The girl collects shells, beach glass, pelican feathers, and messages in bottles. Her mother looks at the water, the sun, the tracks of turtles, the moonlight. In "An Ocean Journal" following the story, the author talks about the treasures she has found on her own familiar beach.

Author/Illustrator Information

Debra Frasier lives in Minneapolis, Minnesota. In addition to *Out of the Ocean,* she is the author/illustrator of the picture book *On the Day You Were Born,* winner of a Parents' Choice award.

Out of the Ocean

by Debra Frasier

Introducing the Book

You may wish to ask children the following questions to **build background** and **introduce story vocabulary.**

- What is an ocean?
- What kinds of sea creatures have shells?
- What is a treasure? What treasures do you have?
- What is a castle?
- What do waves look like?
- When is dawn? How does the day look at dawn?

SETTING A PURPOSE Display the book cover and some of the pages. Remind children that one purpose for reading is to learn. Have children set a purpose for reading. If they have difficulty setting a purpose, offer this suggestion:

> MODEL **The title and pictures show that this book is about the ocean and the beach. I'll read to learn what comes out of the ocean.**

Reading Options

DIRECTED READING Use the Monitor Comprehension questions and Guided Reading strategies on pages 93–94 to check children's comprehension. WHOLE CLASS/SMALL GROUP

INDEPENDENT READING Have children read *Out of the Ocean* and complete the comprehension questions on page 95 independently. Encourage children to write their reactions to the story in their Reading Logs. INDIVIDUAL/WHOLE CLASS

Monitor Comprehension

Use these questions to monitor children's comprehension and evaluate their use of reading strategies.

Pages 2–7

1. **Who are the characters in this book? How can you tell?** (Possible response: a girl and her mother; by the pictures of them) INFERENTIAL: TEXT STRUCTURE
2. **What does the girl's mother ask for every morning?** (Possible response: the sun) INFERENTIAL: IMPORTANT DETAILS
3. **What does the girl's mother ask for from the ocean?** (Possible response: water) INFERENTIAL: IMPORTANT DETAILS

Guided Reading

FOCUS STRATEGY **CREATE MENTAL IMAGES** Have children close their eyes as you reread page 7. Ask what they see in their minds as they make sense of the phrases *water stretches*, *sails above us*, and *clouds bigger than cities*. Ask them what the author means by *water falling into the ocean all over again.* (rain) Explain that when readers picture the words in their minds, they can better understand what they are reading.

Monitor Comprehension

Pages 8–13

4. **How does the girl know she can ask the ocean for shells?** (because every time she goes to the beach, she finds shells) LITERAL: CAUSE-EFFECT
5. **What is the rarest treasure they can find?** (Possible response: red glass rolled smooth and glowing) INFERENTIAL: CLASSIFY
6. **Why is the striped board a surprise?** (It washes in before they asked for it; it was just what they wanted for their castle.) INFERENTIAL: SYNTHESIZE

Guided Reading

FOCUS STRATEGY **USE PICTURE CLUES TO CONFIRM MEANING** Ask children how they can make sure they understand what the girl finds. (She describes things in words, and the pictures show what she is talking about.) Have children look carefully at the pictures to confirm what they read in the text.

Monitor Comprehension

Pages 14–19

7. **What are some of the things the girl finds on the beach?** (Possible responses: pelican feathers, a wooden shoe, floating glass balls, skate egg pouches, plastic boats, abandoned rafts, sea urchin shells, messages in bottles, carved wooden float, coconuts, sea turtle skulls, a beam from a sunken ship, sharks' teeth, a pile of rope) INFERENTIAL: IMPORTANT DETAILS
8. **What does the girl's mother keep asking for?** (sun, water, moonlight, the sound of waves, sea turtle tracks at dawn) LITERAL: NOTE DETAILS
9. **What does the narrator tell her mother?** (Those things are always here. You just have to look for them.) LITERAL: NOTE DETAILS

Guided Reading

MAKE PREDICTIONS Give children the opportunity to predict what will happen in the next part of the selection.

Monitor Comprehension

Pages 20–25

10. **What do the girl and her mother help each other do every day?** (Possible response: remember to see all the big things, too) INFERENTIAL: MAIN IDEA
11. **Why do you think the author wrote this book?** (Possible answer: to help readers see and appreciate what is by the ocean) INFERENTIAL: DETERMINE AUTHOR'S PURPOSE

RETELLING Guidelines for performing a retelling of the story, as well as a rubric for evaluating the retelling, are provided on pages 110–111 of this teacher's guide.

ANSWERS TO COMPREHENSION QUESTIONS ON PAGE 95:

1. (Possible answer: A girl and her mother walk along the beach, build a castle, and talk about what comes out of the ocean: rain, clouds, shells, treasures.) INFERENTIAL: SUMMARIZE
2. (Responses will vary.) CRITICAL: EXPRESS PERSONAL OPINIONS
3. (Possible response: She tells the names of things and shows them in drawings and photographs.) CRITICAL: AUTHOR'S CRAFT

Response to the Literature

WRITING Children should write sentences about a place that is special to them and tell what they can see there if they "remember to look." They should use complete sentences.

Name ______________________________

Out of the Ocean

Answer with complete sentences.

1. What happens in this book?

____

____

____

____

2. What ocean treasure would you like to find? Explain your answer.

____

____

____

3. How does the author help you understand what comes out of the ocean?

____

____

____

RESPONSE TO THE LITERATURE

WRITING Write five sentences about a place that is special to you. Tell what you can see in your special place, if you remember to look. Use complete sentences in your final copy.

Reading Level

Summary

When Cam, her parents, and her friend Eric go to the airport to meet Cam's aunt Molly, they run into a mystery: What happened to Simone, the girl who sat across from Aunt Molly? Her aunt and uncle can't find her, and she doesn't speak English. Cam, using her deductive powers and photographic memory, figures out that Simone has followed someone who looks like her uncle onto the city bus. They find Simone and reunite her with her relatives.

Author Information

David Adler has written more than one hundred books for children, in a variety of genres. He has won many awards, especially for his books about science and history. He tries to alternate between fiction and nonfiction—"I find my fiction to be a wonderful release from all the painstaking research I must do for nonfiction"—and says he has real fun with the Cam Jansen books.

More Books by David Adler

The Babe and I

Calculator Riddles

Cam Jansen and the Catnapping Mystery

The Carsick Zebra and Other Animal Riddles

Cam Jansen and the Mystery of Flight 54

by David A. Adler

Introducing the Book

You may wish to ask children the following questions to **build background** and **introduce story vocabulary.**

- What is a photographic memory?
- What do you do with a camera?
- When do you use luggage?
- What does it mean to be lost?
- What are passengers? When have you been a passenger?
- What kind of announcements might you hear at an airport?
- What is an information desk for?

SETTING A PURPOSE Display the book cover and point out Cam Jansen (the girl). Remind children that one purpose for reading is to be entertained. Have children set a purpose for reading. If they have difficulty setting a purpose, offer this suggestion:

> MODEL **The title and pictures show that this story is about an airline flight. I'll read to find out what the mystery is and how Cam Jansen solves it.**

Reading Options

DIRECTED READING Use the Monitor Comprehension questions and Guided Reading strategies on pages 97–98 to check children's comprehension. WHOLE CLASS/SMALL GROUP

INDEPENDENT READING Have children read *Cam Jansen and the Mystery of Flight 54* and complete the comprehension questions on page 99 independently. Encourage children to write their reactions to the story in their Reading Logs. INDIVIDUAL/WHOLE CLASS

Monitor Comprehension

Use these questions to monitor children's comprehension and evaluate their use of reading strategies.

Pages 1–13

1. **Cam's real name is Jennifer. Why is she called Cam?** (*Cam* is short for *The Camera*, her nickname because she has a photographic memory and says *click* like a camera when she uses it.) LITERAL: IDENTIFY CHARACTER TRAITS
2. **Why is Cam Jansen in the airport?** (Possible response: to pick up her aunt Molly) INFERENTIAL: CAUSE-EFFECT
3. **What problem does Aunt Molly discover?** (Possible response: She has the wrong suitcase.) INFERENTIAL: DRAW CONCLUSIONS

Guided Reading

FOCUS STRATEGY **REREAD** Ask children what they can do if they forget a detail or realize they don't understand what they've read. (reread to find information they may have missed before)

Monitor Comprehension

Pages 14–27

4. **Why does Aunt Molly take the wrong suitcase?** (Possible response: It looks like hers, and she forgets she had used her larger suitcase.) INFERENTIAL: CAUSE-EFFECT
5. **Why are the Greens worried about Simone?** (Possible responses: She's their niece; she was on Flight 54 but they can't find her; she doesn't speak English.) INFERENTIAL: DETERMINE CHARACTERS' EMOTIONS
6. **What do you think will happen next?** (Responses will vary.) INFERENTIAL: MAKE PREDICTIONS

Guided Reading

FOCUS STRATEGY **CREATE MENTAL IMAGES** Have children look for details about the airport in Chapter 4. Ask them what details the author uses to help readers see (the guard, service desk, Jill Waner, luggage); hear (announcements, pages); taste or smell (popcorn). Explain that the author gives these details to help readers better understand what they are reading.

Monitor Comprehension

Pages 28–42

7. **Why does Eric think Simone will be in a restaurant?** (Possible response: He thinks she may have been hungry after the flight, because Aunt Molly was.) INFERENTIAL: DRAW CONCLUSIONS

8. **Why does Cam chase the girl on the elevator?** (Possible response: The girl looks like Simone.) INFERENTIAL: DRAW CONCLUSIONS

9. **When does Cam use her photographic memory? Hint: Look back for *"Click."*** (Possible response: when she sees a photograph of Simone; when she sees people running for a bus; when she's leaving the airport) INFERENTIAL: TEXT STRUCTURE

10. **Where does Cam think they will find Simone?** (Possible response: at a city bus stop) INFERENTIAL: IMPORTANT DETAILS

Guided Reading

MAKE PREDICTIONS Give children the opportunity to predict what will happen in the next part of the selection.

Monitor Comprehension

Pages 43–56

11. **How does following the wrong girl help Cam find Simone?** (Possible response: She figures out that Simone might have followed someone.) CRITICAL: INTERPRET STORY EVENTS

12. **How are Aunt Molly and Cam different?** (Possible answer: Cam notices and remembers things; Aunt Molly mixes up her suitcases and her relatives' names, and she forgets things like her birthday.) INFERENTIAL: COMPARE AND CONTRAST

RETELLING Guidelines for performing a retelling of the story, as well as a rubric for evaluating the retelling, are provided on pages 110–111 of this teacher's guide.

ANSWERS TO COMPREHENSION QUESTIONS ON PAGE 99:

1. (Possible response: Cam uses her photographic memory to picture Simone. Then she watches people running for the city bus and thinks Simone may have tried to follow someone who looked like her uncle and gotten on the bus. Cam gets her dad to follow the bus until they see Simone at a bus stop.) INFERENTIAL: SUMMARIZE

2. (Responses will vary.) CRITICAL: EXPRESS PERSONAL OPINIONS

3. (Possible response: Cam is smart and uses her brain. She notices things. She has a photographic memory.) CRITICAL: AUTHOR'S CRAFT

Response to the Literature

WRITING Children should write letters to Cam Jansen from Mr. or Mrs. Green. Their letters should thank Cam for helping find Simone and tell how they felt when Simone was found. Children should use complete sentences and a letter format.

Name ______________________

Cam Jansen and the Mystery of Flight 54

Answer with complete sentences.

1. How does Cam Jansen solve the mystery of Flight 54?

2. Do you like to read mystery stories? Why or why not?

3. What character traits help Cam Jansen solve mysteries?

RESPONSE TO THE LITERATURE

WRITING Imagine that you are Mr. or Mrs. Green. Write a letter to Cam Jansen to thank her for finding Simone. Tell how you felt when Simone was found. Use complete sentences in your letter.

Reading Level

Summary

Martin Luther King, Jr., was born in Atlanta, Georgia, in 1929. He was a good student who became a pastor and a leader. He worked hard to change the laws so that all people, regardless of race, could sit where they wanted on buses and share the same restaurants, drinking fountains, and schools. He was shot and killed in 1968. Every year, he is honored on his birthday, Martin Luther King Day.

Author Information

Jean Marzollo has written more than sixty books for children, young adults, and adults. In an autobiographical essay, she wrote: "When I write books for beginning readers . . . I remember what I liked to read at that age—exciting books that made me feel both happy and sad and that taught me something."

Illustrator Information

J. Brian Pinkney is known for his scratch board illustration technique. He has illustrated many books by many well-known writers and has won the Parents' Choice Picture Book Award three times.

More books by Jean Marzollo

Baseball Brothers

Cannonball Chris

How Kids Grow

Happy Birthday, Martin Luther King

by Jean Marzollo

Introducing the Book

You may wish to ask children the following questions to **build background** and **introduce story vocabulary.**

- Why do people go to college?
- Where does a pastor or minister work?
- What does it mean to "live in peace"?
- What does it mean to be famous?
- Why are laws important?
- How can someone show that he or she has leadership ability?
- What is justice?
- When might someone give a speech?

SETTING A PURPOSE Display the book cover and point out Martin Luther King, Jr. Remind children that one purpose for reading is to learn. Have children set a purpose for reading. If they have difficulty setting a purpose, offer this suggestion:

MODEL **The title tells me this book is about Martin Luther King. I'll read to find out who he was and why we remember his birthday.**

Reading Options

DIRECTED READING Use the Monitor Comprehension questions and Guided Reading strategies on pages 101–102 to check children's comprehension. WHOLE CLASS/SMALL GROUP

INDEPENDENT READING Have children read *Happy Birthday, Martin Luther King* and complete the comprehension questions on page 103 independently. Encourage children to write their reactions to the story in their Reading Logs. INDIVIDUAL/WHOLE CLASS

Monitor Comprehension

Use these questions to monitor children's comprehension and evaluate their use of reading strategies.

Pages 2–9

1. **When was Martin Luther King, Jr., born?** (January 15, 1929) LITERAL: NOTE DETAILS
2. **Whom was Martin Luther King, Jr., named after?** (Possible response: his father) INFERENTIAL: IMPORTANT DETAILS
3. **What did Martin study to be?** (Possible response: a pastor) INFERENTIAL: IMPORTANT DETAILS

Guided Reading

FOCUS STRATEGY **REREAD** Ask children what they can do if they forget a detail or realize they don't understand what they've read. (go back and reread to find what they missed) Point out that rereading is an important strategy to use when reading nonfiction books.

Monitor Comprehension

Pages 10–15

4. **What are some things that Martin did as a minister?** (Possible response: visited sick people, asked people not to fight with each other, led people in prayer and song) INFERENTIAL: SUMMARIZE
5. **What did Martin say about problems?** (He said that there were peaceful ways to solve problems.) LITERAL: IDENTIFY CHARACTERS' EMOTIONS
6. **What do you think Martin was like?** (Possible answer: caring, brave) INFERENTIAL: DETERMINE CHARACTERS' TRAITS

Guided Reading

FOCUS STRATEGY **SELF-CORRECT** Tell children that sometimes when they read a word and it doesn't make sense, they might notice that the letters in the word do not match the way they have read it. Have children correct themselves when this happens by looking carefully at the word and rereading it.

Monitor Comprehension

Pages 16–21

7. **Why is Martin Luther King, Jr., famous?** (He helped our country change some of its laws.) LITERAL: CAUSE-EFFECT
8. **What did the old laws say?** (Possible response: African Americans could sit only at the back of a bus and could use only certain restaurants and drinking fountains; they could not go to school with other people.) INFERENTIAL: SUMMARIZE
9. **What do the new laws say?** (Possible response: Anyone can sit in any seat; all people can use the same restaurants and drinking fountains; everyone can go to school together.) INFERENTIAL: SUMMARIZE

Guided Reading

MAKE PREDICTIONS Give children the opportunity to predict what they will learn about Martin Luther King, Jr., in the next part of the selection.

Monitor Comprehension

Pages 22–28

10. **What did Martin Luther King, Jr., do that made him special?** (Possible response: He was able to make people listen and work with him for justice.) INFERENTIAL: DETERMINE CHARACTERS' TRAITS
11. **What did he say in 1963, in his most famous speech?** (Possible responses: He asked the President for jobs and freedom for African Americans. He said he had a dream that people everywhere could learn to live together without being mean to each other.) INFERENTIAL: SUMMARIZE
12. **What happened after he died?** (Possible responses: People were very sad. They marched in a parade and buried him with a special gravestone. His birthday became a holiday.) INFERENTIAL: SEQUENCE

RETELLING Guidelines for performing a retelling of the story, as well as a rubric for evaluating the retelling, are provided on pages 110–111 of this teacher's guide.

ANSWERS TO COMPREHENSION QUESTIONS ON PAGE 103:

1. (Possible response: He helped change laws so that African Americans would be treated fairly and could do all the things other people could do.) INFERENTIAL: SUMMARIZE
2. (Responses will vary.) CRITICAL: EXPRESS PERSONAL OPINIONS
3. (Possible response: The words tell about the life of Martin Luther King, Jr. The pictures help readers understand what he did and show how people remember him.) CRITICAL: INTERPRET TEXT STRUCTURE

Response to the Literature

WRITING Children should write sentences about Martin Luther King, Jr. They should use their own words to tell why he is famous and what he did to help people. They should use complete sentences.

Name ______________________________

Happy Birthday, Martin Luther King

Answer with complete sentences.

1. What did Martin Luther King, Jr., do to help people in our country?

____

____

____

2. Why do you think people still remember the speech Martin Luther King, Jr., made in 1963?

____

____

____

3. How does this book help people learn about Martin Luther King, Jr.?

____

____

____

RESPONSE TO THE LITERATURE

WRITING Write a paragraph about Martin Luther King, Jr. Use your own words to tell readers about him. Tell why he is famous. Tell what he did to help people. Use complete sentences.

Individual Reading Inventory Form

Student: ______________________________ Date: ________________________

Selection Title: *The Best Friends Club*, pages 16–17 Word Count: 98

The next day Harold came out of his classroom with Douglas again.

"Douglas asked me to play at his house," said Harold.

"*Harold*," said Lizzie. "What about the club?"

"What club?" asked Douglas.

"None of your business," said Lizzie.

"I'll come tomorrow," said Harold. "I promise."

Lizzie watched them walk away together. She stuck out her tongue at them, but Harold didn't turn around.

She went straight to the clubhouse and wrote down another rule. It said

7. Best friends don't go to other people's houses to play.

Then she threw a ball at the garage wall until suppertime.

Comments: ____

____

____

Indicate correct (+) or incorrect (-) response for each question:

1. **What does Harold promise Lizzie?** (that he will come to the club tomorrow)
2. **What rule does Lizzie write down?** (Best friends don't go to other people's houses to play.)
3. **Why does Lizzie stick her tongue out at Harold and Douglas?** (She is mad at them.)
4. **Why do you think Lizzie throws a ball at the garage wall?** (She is hurt and angry and feels left out.)

Individual Reading Inventory Summary Form

Student: ____________________ Grade: ________ Date: ________

Passage: ____________________ Word Count: ________

1. Miscues

Total number of miscues _______

Meaning-based miscues _______

Graphic/sound-based miscues _______

Comments and patterns observed: ____

____

Total number of self-corrections _______

Comments and patterns observed: ____

____

Error Rate

- Subtract the number of self-corrections from the total number of miscues for a subtotal.
- Divide the subtotal by the word count of the passage.

______________ ÷ ______________ = ______________

(SUBTOTAL) (WORD COUNT) ERROR RATE

2. Fluency

Number of words read per minute _______

______________ ÷ ______________ = ______________

(NUMBER OF CORRECT WORDS READ PER MINUTE) (WORD COUNT) FLUENCY RATE

Comments and patterns observed: ____

____

3. Comprehension

______________ ÷ **4 X 100** = ______________%

(TOTAL CORRECT ANSWERS) COMPREHENSION SCORE

Comments and patterns observed: ____

____

Summary Comments

Individual Reading Inventory Form

Student: ______________________________ Date: ______________________

Selection Title: *Alistair in Outer Space*, pages 8–15 Word Count: 106

One day, when Alistair was returning his books to the library, something unusual happened.

He was picked up by a space ship and whisked off into space.

Two creatures who called themselves Goots were flying the space ship. They were from a planet known as Gootula. They were very friendly.

The Goots liked Alistair very much and wanted to take him home with them.

Alistar thanked the Goots very much. But he did not want to go to Gootula. "My library books are due back today," he said. "The librarian will be expecting me."

The Goots pretended not to hear Alistair and continued on their way.

Comments: ______________________________

____

____

Indicate correct (+) or incorrect (-) response for each question:

1. **What happens to Alistair when he is returning his books to the library?** (He is picked up by a space ship.)
2. **Who is flying the space ship?** (two creatures called Goots)
3. **Why doesn't Alistair want to go to Gootula?** (His library books are due.)
4. **Why do you think the Goots pretend they can't hear Alistair?** (They want to take him to Gootula.)

Individual Reading Inventory Summary Form

Student: ____________________ Grade: ________ Date: ________

Passage: ____________________ Word Count: ________

1. Miscues

Total number of miscues ________

Meaning-based miscues ________

Graphic/sound-based miscues ________

Comments and patterns observed: ______________________________

____

Total number of self-corrections ________

Comments and patterns observed: ______________________________

____

Error Rate

- Subtract the number of self-corrections from the total number of miscues for a subtotal.
- Divide the subtotal by the word count of the passage.

______________ ÷ ______________ = ______________

(SUBTOTAL) (WORD COUNT) ERROR RATE

2. Fluency

Number of words read per minute ________

______________ ÷ ______________ = ______________

(NUMBER OF CORRECT WORDS READ PER MINUTE) (WORD COUNT) FLUENCY RATE

Comments and patterns observed: ______________________________

____

3. Comprehension

______________ ÷ **4 X 100** = ______________%

(TOTAL CORRECT ANSWERS) COMPREHENSION SCORE

Comments and patterns observed: ______________________________

____

Summary Comments

Individual Reading Inventory Form

Student: ______________________________ Date: ________________________

Selection Title: *Emergency!*, pages 12–15 Word Count: 109

Emergency! Fire trucks rush to a fire. Different types of fire trucks are used to fight different kinds of fires.

Tanker trucks can fight fires as soon as they arrive at the scene. They carry their own water supply. The fire fighters pump the water through hoses onto the fire.

Pumper trucks don't carry their own water. Instead, they pump water from a fire hydrant or other water sources, such as ponds, lakes, or rivers. The water goes into the trucks through hoses. The pumps in the fire trucks push the water back out of the trucks and up through the discharge hoses. Streams of water hit the flames.

Comments: ____

____

____

Indicate correct (+) or incorrect (-) response for each question:

1. **Which kind of fire trucks carry their own water?** (tanker trucks)
2. **Where do pumper trucks pump water from?** (fire hydrants, ponds, lakes, or rivers)
3. **Which kind of truck can probably start fighting a fire first?** (a tanker truck)
4. **When might a tanker truck be sent to a fire instead of a pumper truck?** (when there is no fire hydrant or other water source nearby)

Individual Reading Inventory Summary Form

Student: ____________________ Grade: ________ Date: ________

Passage: ____________________ Word Count: ________

1. Miscues

Total number of miscues _______

Meaning-based miscues _______

Graphic/sound-based miscues _______

Comments and patterns observed: ____

____

Total number of self-corrections _______

Comments and patterns observed: ____

____

Error Rate

- Subtract the number of self-corrections from the total number of miscues for a subtotal.
- Divide the subtotal by the word count of the passage.

______________ ÷ ______________ = ______________

(SUBTOTAL) **(WORD COUNT)** **ERROR RATE**

2. Fluency

Number of words read per minute _______

______________ ÷ ______________ = ______________

(NUMBER OF CORRECT WORDS READ PER MINUTE) **(WORD COUNT)** **FLUENCY RATE**

Comments and patterns observed: ____

____

3. Comprehension

______________ ÷ **4 X 100** = ______________%

(TOTAL CORRECT ANSWERS) **COMPREHENSION SCORE**

Comments and patterns observed: ____

____

Summary Comments

Using Retelling to Assess Comprehension

Retelling

Retelling is an assessment strategy that may be used to measure a student's strengths and weaknesses in comprehension. Listening to a retelling provides insights into a student's ability to construct meaning, to identify important information, to make inferences, and to organize and summarize information. Specifically, listening to a retelling can help you assess whether the student

- relates the main idea and relevant details in sequence
- provides a summarizing statement
- includes story elements
- uses phrases, language, or vocabulary from the text
- evaluates an author's point of view, purpose, or craft
- stays on topic
- understands relationships in the text
- provides extensions of the text
- relates text to relevant experiences

Oral Retelling

When conducting an oral retelling, ask students to tell the story in their own words. Try not to interrupt. Allow plenty of time for a student to complete an oral retelling, and be sure the student has nothing more to say before ending the session.

For the emerging reader who is reading books with limited text, the retelling may be short and fairly simple: adjust criteria in the attached rubric as necessary. For more complex books, if a student needs prompting, try using generic statements such as "Tell me more," "Keep going," and "You're doing a good job." If you need to elicit more information, prompt the student by asking open-ended questions such as these:

- What was the character's main problem?
- What was your favorite part of the story?
- Where did the story take place?
- Who else was in the story?
- How did the story end?
- What else do you remember from the story?

Written Retelling

When conducting a written retelling, ask students to tell the story in their own words and not to worry about spelling or handwriting. Try to allow plenty of time for students to complete writing before ending the session.

Use the rubric on the following page to assess oral and written retellings.

Scoring Rubric for Retellings

<table>
<tr><th>SCORE</th><th>CHARACTERISTICS</th></tr>
<tr><td>3</td><td>Proficient: Student retells the text using complex responses that demonstrate a thorough understanding and interpretation of the text.<ul><li>relates the main idea and important and supporting details</li><li>relates text in sequence</li><li>provides a summarizing statement</li><li>includes story elements such as setting, characters, plot, problems, and resolutions</li><li>uses phrases, language, vocabulary, sentence structure, or literary devices from the text</li><li>evaluates the author's point of view, purpose, or craft</li><li>stays on topic</li><li>discriminates between reality and fantasy, fact and fiction</li><li>understands relationships in text such as cause and effect</li><li>classifies, groups, compares, or contrasts information</li><li>provides extensions of the text, such as making connections to other texts, relating relevant experiences, or making generalizations</li></ul></td></tr>
<tr><td>2</td><td>Satisfactory: Student adequately retells the text and demonstrates an understanding of the text.<ul><li>relates the main idea and relevant details</li><li>relates most of the text in sequence</li><li>includes story elements such as setting, characters, main problem, and resolution</li><li>uses language or vocabulary from the text</li><li>stays on topic</li><li>discriminates between reality and fantasy</li><li>understands relationships in text such as cause and effect</li><li>classifies, groups, compares, or contrasts information</li><li>provides some extensions of the text, such as making connections to other texts or relating relevant experiences</li></ul></td></tr>
<tr><td>1</td><td>Minimal: Student makes several inaccurate, incomplete, or irrelevant statements or otherwise provides evidence of lack of comprehension.<ul><li>misunderstands main idea and omits important details</li><li>relates text out of sequence</li><li>omits story elements or provides incorrect information about setting, characters, and plot</li><li>provides a poorly organized or unclear structure</li><li>provides no extensions of the text</li></ul></td></tr>
</table>